D0946305

ÙW Library BOOK SALE

U.W. Library BOOK SALE

Nietzsche in German Politics and Society
1890–1918

Nietzsche in German Politics and Society 1890–1918

R. Hinton Thomas

OPEN COURT

La Salle, Illinois

OPEN COURT and the above logo are registered in the U.S. Patent and Trademark
Office. © 1983 by Richard Hinton Thomas. All rights reserved. No part of
this publication may be reproduced, stored in a retrieval system, or trans-
mitted, in any form or by any means, electronic, mechanical, photocopying,
recording, or otherwise, without the prior written permission of the publisher,
Open Court Publishing Company, La Salle, Illinois 61301.
First published by Manchester University Press, 1983. This edition: 1986.
Printed and bound in the United States of America.
0C865   10 9 8 7 6 5 4 3 2 1
ISBN: 0-8126-9003-6

Library of Congress Cataloging in Publication Data

Thomas, R. Hinton (Richard Hinton), 1912–
    Nietzsche in German politics and society, 1890–1918.

    Bibliography: p.
    Includes index.
    1. Nietzsche, Friedrich Wilhelm, 1844–1900—Influence.
    2. Germany—Politics and government—1888–1918.
    3. Germany—Social conditions.   I. Title.
    B3317.T54   1985   320.5′0943   85-8961
    ISBN 0-8126-9003-6

Contents

Foreword

The research necessary for the writing of this book was begun with the assistance of a study grant from the German Academic Exchange Service, to which I must here express my gratitude. Thereafter I was decisively dependent on generous financial help from the British Academy, to which, therefore, my very special thanks are due.

I am pleased too to recall the facilities made available to me by the International Institute of Social History in Amsterdam, the Library of the Freie Universität, Berlin, the Archiv der Deutschen Jugendbewegung at Burg Ludwigstein, the Bundesarchiv at Koblenz, the Institut für Zeitungsgeschichte at Dortmund, the Zentralinstitut für Soziale Fragen in Berlin and the Diederichs Verlag, Cologne. I owe a debt of gratitude to Herr Ulf Diederichs who not only gave permission for me to work in the archive of his publishing house, but also greatly assisted me while I was there, and to Dr Winfried Mogge, Archivdirektor at Burg Ludwigstein, who likewise devoted a great deal of time to helping me. Professor R. J. Evans kindly allowed me to draw on his expert knowledge of the German feminist movement and also made available to me archival material which I should not otherwise have been able to consult. I must also not fail to mention how much I gained from discussions with Roger Fletcher, whose doctoral research in the Department of History at Brisbane University was of great value to me as regards one particular chapter. Finally, I must gratefully remember Professor J. A. S. Grenville's kindness in reading through the whole of my typescript, as a result of which I was able to improve the text in a number of different and significant ways.

I owe a word of thanks also to the editors of *Oxford German Studies* and *German Life and Letters* for allowing me, in the case of Chapter VI and the Appendix, to reproduce modified versions of articles already published in these journals.

RHT

Introduction

Immediately after the Second World War, when in the interests of denazification Germans were being investigated for their involvement in National Socialism and their suitability or otherwise for holding a job, there was the case of Ernst Bertram, author of a distinguished book on Nietzsche. This helped to make him immediately suspect, for Nietzsche was then in very bad repute. One did not need to have read, least of all understood, anything that he had written to know that he was the philosopher of 'will to power', champion of the Superman (commonly imagined as a sort of cross between a muscular Mr World and Flash Gordon), and exponent of the notion that the world was best served by encouraging the strong and neglecting the weak. So, on the face of it there was an obvious correlation between Nietzsche's thinking and the ethos of the Great Dictator.

During the First World War, moreover, Nietzsche had often been regarded, particularly in England, as having helped to cause it. Books and articles were written to this effect, and the idea had got about that Nietzsche was of the same ilk as nationalists, militarists and warmongers such as General Friedrich von Bernhardi and the historian Heinrich von Treitschke. All the more, therefore, was there a temptation after 1945 to include him among the guilty men of Germany's philosophical past. The Nazis had idolised him, Alfred Rosenberg had praised him in *Der Mythus des 20. Jahrhunderts*, and a much publicised photograph had shown Hitler gazing with respectful solemnity at Nietzsche's bust in the Nietzsche Archive in Weimar.

The ill-fame that had thus become associated with Nietzsche's name had retrospective consequences. It affected the image of the part he had played in his own time and helped to strengthen the belief that his influence had been to encourage the more brutal features of Wilhelmine Germany. It came to be assumed that it was their exponents who had most admired Nietzsche and derived the greatest encouragement from his ideas, and that it was those on the democratic and humanitarian side who had wanted to have least to do with him.

However, while a lot has been written about Nietzsche's significance as far as literature is concerned, relatively little attention has been paid to his influence on people practically engaged in the world of politics and society. In judging Nietzsche's effect in, as one might say, the real world, they are what really matters. It is the aim of this book to make good the omission, and the result will be to transfer the emphasis from Nietzsche as a factor behind power-political and repressive attitudes to what, for example, Herbert Marcuse, philosopher and friend of radical democracy, came to regard as the liberating atmosphere of his thinking.

Nietzsche's active career as a writer spans almost exactly the age of Bismarck. His first major work, *The Birth of Tragedy*, was begun during the Franco-Prussian war and *The Twilight of the Idols*, the last to be completed prior to his final breakdown, appeared the year before the Chancellor's dismissal, in 1889. During that period, however, his influence was relatively limited. The decisive change took place at just about the time when Bismarck's period of office ended. It happened quickly and quite dramatically.

Hitherto, interest in Nietzsche's work had been restricted, individuals apart, to a few coteries, such as the Pernestorfer circle in Vienna,[1] the Olden circle in Weimar,[2] the Dehmel circle, and the group founded in 1886 in Berlin known as 'Durch'.[3] Then, fairly suddenly, he began to reach a much broader public.[4] If one had to settle for a single year from which to date this transformation, 1890 would be the one to choose. This was the year after Nietzsche's collapse in Turin, so when at last he became widely known and talked about, he himself, ironically, was oblivious to what was going on.

The change reflected itself very clearly in two of the most important journals of the time, *Die Gesellschaft* and the *Freie Bühne* (later called *Die neue Rundschau*). One has only to turn their pages to be struck by the new and lively interest being taken in Nietzsche from that point onwards. There, and elsewhere, frequent statements testified to this new and exciting development. Nietzsche 'was well on the way to becoming the fashionable philosopher',[5] the 'great event of the time'. His 'invisible rays' were penetrating 'into the remotest areas'.[6] He had stepped 'out of the darkness into the bright light of day'.[7] When in 1892 an advertisement appeared for a new book on Nietzsche, it played on the idea that 'the whole cultural world is stirred' by his importance.[8] 'Naturally Nietzsche was discussed', someone remarked about a meeting of a cultural society which he had just attended, for where 'would one not now be talking about Nietzsche?'[9] By 1895 'the number of his followers is increasing every day'.[10]

This sudden popularity, it is important to note, came in the context of Germany's rapidly advancing industrialisation. Developing fast during the 1890s, it soared to a high point in about 1890. For many people, the result was to make society appear massive and impersonal. How to be true to one's natural self, in conditions hostile to *Individualität* and *Persönlichkeit*, was more and more the problem.[11] These terms became constantly recurring motifs in the cultural debate, their distinctive overtones in German lending them magical, even metaphysical associations which translation can too easily fail to convey. Their loss and recovery was a central preoccupation, for example, of Julius Langbehn's best-selling *Rembrandt als Erzieher*, the first of many editions of which appeared in 1890. Symptomatic too, and intellectually more significant, was the reception of Nietzsche as the philosopher of self-release. Quoted over and over again was his call to 'become what you are', known mainly for its appearance in *Thus spake Zarathustra*. This was by far the most popular and influential of his books, and the one that most people who knew anything at all about him had at least dipped into, even if they had read nothing else. It is remarkable how often, when it is quoted, the references are to the earlier, and in some ways easier, parts of the book, as if that was as far as the reader had got. There is a cry on all sides, it was remarked, for *Individualität*, and a close connection was noted between ideas of *Individualität* and *Persönlichkeit* and the 'young race of Zarathustra'.[12] 'The individual', it was stated in 1895, 'has become conscious of himself ... This is the liberating achievement we owe to Nietzsche.'[13] When, however, to mention a case typical of many, Rudolf Steiner discovered Nietzsche for himself in 1889, the effect was to nourish views of his own, to which he had come 'independently and by other means'.[14] This was a common experience. Spengler in his early days illustrates it too. He had all long been an 'aristocrat', he said, and 'I took Nietzsche for granted before knowing anything of his work'.[15]

Thus, from around 1890 Nietzsche became for the first time a figure of major general importance. This applied not merely to writers and intellectuals. It included also people directly and predominantly involved in social and political activities, and our first example will illustrate this by reference to the protest movement of the so-called *Jungen* within the Social Democratic Party.

This raises the question, important in this particular connection, as to how Nietzsche of all people could possibly be attractive to anyone on the left. He was, after all, a declared enemy of socialism and spoke of it with contempt. Egalitarianism of any sort was anathema to him. What he championed above all was the aristocratic principle. This might seem to rule him out of court, as far as socialists were concerned. Things, however, were not quite as simple as that.

Already in the *Untimely Meditations* he had campaigned against the kind of hyprocrisy and idealistic make-believe which journals such as *Die Gesellschaft* and the *Freie Bühne*, with their socialistic leanings, were to condemn as essentially bourgeois. Like any socialist, it could be said, he set his sights on a finer future and a worthier type of man. He called on people not to be led astray by the 'masking of physiological needs in the guise of ... the ideal, the purely spiritual'.[16] There was common ground here with an attitude to life which rested on a materialist philosophy and a belief, shared with Zarathustra, in the need to 'remain true to the earth', to 'serve the meaning of the earth'.[17] Socialism could learn from Nietzsche, one read in the socialist press; Nietzsche and socialism belong together. What applies to the one, it was argued, applies to the other, each is 'revolutionary', each 'pregnant with the future'.[18] There was the case, for example, of Friedrich Wolf, later well known as a writer and a communist. As a young man, he was an enthusiastic reader of Nietzsche — at least of *Also sprach Zarathustra* — at the same time as he was becoming interested in socialism.[19]

But what of Nietzsche's bitter criticism of socialism? Even this could have its uses from a socialist point of view in certain circumstances. Nietzsche had said that socialism subordinated individuality to ideology and the collective. When, therefore, there were some within the party who viewed it as a mass organisation crushing the individual will and ruled dictatorially by an older generation with ossified values, Nietzsche was at hand to encourage them.

At around this time, moreover, and especially among people who believed, however vaguely and romantically, in a socialist future, a sense of fresh beginnings and fresh hope was often expressed. Newness (*das Neue*) is all around us, ran an enthusiastic comment in the *Freie Bühne*, and 'the time we are moving into is rich in possibilities'.[20] 'The young generation ... has now taken command', it was being said in *Die Gesellschaft*.[21] The death of the old Kaiser, the advent of a 'youthful emperor filled with high endeavour and bold idealism', the dismissal of an ageing chancellor, the promise of the *Neue Kurs*, and the perspectives opened by the lifting of the Anti-Socialist Law — all these were elements in the situation. 'The splendours of the 1890s' was how one young socialist of the time would describe those years in retrospect. A sense of 'growth and development (*neues Werden*)', he recalled, combined with the 'youth of those experiencing it' to generate expectation and confidence.[22]

In this association of politics and youth the idea of the working class played a significant part. As a late development in the history of social change, it could easily be felt to have the future on its side. Unlike the bourgeoisie after 1848, experience had not disappointed it. Its values were untarnished, its principles uncompromised. 'The youthful force of the working-class world' over and against the senility of capitalism[23] — that was how the situation looked to one observer, implying a latent energy which, released and encouraged, could shape a future closer to the heart's desire.

From this point of view, a younger generation of socialists, fastening attention on the enemy within, was all the more tempted to see as the barrier the cramping authoritarianism in the party of an older generation, too bureaucratic in its attitudes, too unhurried in its time-scale of change, lacking in any sense of urgency, too easily prone to want to let things take their course. In short, as they saw it, it was too indifferent to the creative force of feeling, energy and the will — and in these terms Nietzsche was a natural ally of the critics.

This, briefly sketched, was the background against which the *Jungen*, as they came to be known, went into the attack under the banner of youth, master-minded by a man whose intellectual heroes included no one to whom he was more indebted than to Nietzsche. We have now, therefore, to consider the course of events, what Nietzsche meant to him, why, and with what effect.

Notes to Introduction

[1] For a detailed discussion of this important group and the part that Nietzsche played in it, cf. William J. McGrath, *Dionysian Art and Populist Politics in Austria* (New Haven and London, 1974).

[2] Briefly described in Rudolf Steiner, *Mein Lebensgang* (Dornach, 1962).

[3] For a short account, cf. Katharina Günther, *Literarische Gruppenbildung im Berliner Naturalismus* (Berlin, 1972).

[4] In this connection cf. Gisela Diesz, *Die Entwicklung des Nietzsche-Bildes in Deutschland* (Würzburg, 1933).

[5] Paul Ernst, 'Friedrich Nietzsche: Seine Philosophie', in *Freie Bühne* (1890), p. 516.

[6] Max Halbe, *Scholle und Schicksal* (Salzburg, 1940), pp. 369 ff.

[7] Heinrich Hart, 'Wir Westfalen', in *Gesammelte Werke*, III (Berlin, 1907), p. 87.

[8] *Die Gesellschaft*, February 1892.

[9] O. E. Hartleben, *Tagebuch: Fragmente eines Lebens* (Munich, 1906), pp. 117–9. The reference is to the Menschenklub in Magdeburg.

[10] Cf. Karl Joel, 'Das Zeitalter der Ethik', in *Neue deutsche Rundschau/Freie Bühne*, p. 107. For a survey of references to Nietzsche in newspapers and journals, cf. Joëlle Philippi, *Das Nietzsche-Bild in der deutschen Zeitschriftenpresse der Jahrhundertwende* (unpublished dissertation, Saarbrucken, 1970).

[11] As to why, cf. the suggestive, if controversial, essays by Hans Speier, 'Zur Soziologie der bürgerlichen Intelligenz in Deutschland', and Gert Mattenklott, 'Nietzsches "Geburt der Tragödie" als Konzept einer bürgerlichen Kulturrevolution', in Gert Mattenklott and Klaus R. Scherpe (eds.), *Positionen der literarischen Intelligenz zwischen bürgerlicher Reaktion und Imperialismus* (Kronberg/Ts., 1973).

[12] Leo Berg, 'Die Individualität', later included in his *Zwischen zwei Jahrhunderten* (Frankfurt am Main, 1896).

[13] Franz Servaes, in *Neue deutsche Rundschau/Freie Bühne* (1895), p. 166. Cf. also, among many other examples, Theobald Ziegler, 'Auf der Schwelle des neuen Jahrhunderts', in *ibid.* (1900), pp. 1 ff.

[14] Rudolf Steiner, Preface to his *Friedrich Nietzsche: ein Kämpfer gegen seine Zeit* (Weimar, 1895).

[15] Quoted in A. M. Koktanek, *Oswald Spengler in seiner Zeit* (Munich, 1968), p. 53.

[16] Werke, ed. Schlechta, II, p. 11.

[17] *Ibid.*, II, pp. 280, 328.

[18] Franz Servaes, 'Nietzsche und der Sozialismus', in *Freie Bühne* (1892), pp. 85 ff.

[19] Cf. Walther Pollatschek, *Friedrich Wolf* (Berlin, 1963), pp. 20–21.

[20] Preface to the *Freie Bühne* (1892), p. 2.

[21] Conrad Alberti, 'Der tote Kaiser', in *Die Gesellschaft* (1889), p. 766.

[22] Letter of Josef Bloch to Hugo Leuthner of 31 March 1910, in the Bundesarchiv, Koblenz, reference: *Sozialistische Monatshefte* R 117/8 fol 1.

[23] Max Nettlau Archiv, in the International Institute of Social History, Amsterdam: MS. 1895–1914, p. 134.

I

Social Democracy, the Jungen and Nietzsche

The Sozialistische Partei Deutschlands (SPD) dates effectively from the fusion of separate groups in the socialist movement at Gotha in 1875, with August Bebel as the dominant figure, and from 1876 *Vorwärts* as the party paper.

The Anti-Socialist Law of 1878 meant that its public existence was proscribed. Representation in the Reichstag, however, was still allowed, and between 1878 and the end of that legislation in 1890 the SPD gained massively at the polls. It outstripped all other parties, with roughly twenty per cent of the votes, though, as a result of the electoral system, it secured only thirty-five seats in the Reichstag. That was one consequence of the Anti-Socialist Law. Another was to influence the party to overstep the limits of the Gotha programme. This had laid down that its objectives were to be pursued within the framework of legality. There was now increasing support for the idea of using whatever means seemed necessary. This helped to radicalise the working class, to popularise in its ranks the writings of Marx and Engels, and to make it more receptive to the idea that the working class alone could bring about its own emancipation. Though the Erfurt programme of 1890 proclaimed a more dogmatically Marxist line, the growth of the SPD after the lifting of the Anti-Socialist Law served to foster in some quarters more patient, compromising attitudes. These were represented among others by Georg von Vollmar and culminated in the revisionist movement, associated above all with Eduard Bernstein.

While the leadership of the party was now inclined to attitudes that were less than radical, elements of the working class itself were, to a significant extent, drawn to more direct forms of action. Against the background of this cleavage of opinion the party was faced with an important decision. As things now stood, was its aim to be revolution or should its policy be one of gradual change on a parliamentary basis? Especially some of the younger generation, notably in the areas with the densest working class population such as Dresden, Magdeburg and Berlin, tended to think the latter too slow and ineffectual. A group, led by Bruno Wille, instigated a counter-campaign, and it was this group which became known as the *Jungen*. None of them were, strictly speaking, proletarian. Two, Wilhelm Werner and Karl Wildberger, were craftsmen, while others, like Wille himself, could best be described as intellectuals, a fact which gave Engels the chance to sneer at the affair[1] as a 'revolt of literati and students'.[2]

Two issues were of particular importance. One concerned the question of May Day. It had been decided at the opening meeting of the Second International at Paris in 1889 that the following year the first of May should everywhere be an occasion for mass demonstrations by the working class. The party leadership in Germany was against the idea and expressed its disapproval by refraining from giving any lead in that direction. In the event, the occasion passed off quietly in Germany, though a large number of workers in Hamburg, for example, were known to have wanted to make the day a public holiday, and the Berlin Social Democrats had declared themselves in favour.[3] To Wille it was plain that the leadership was dragging its feet and frustrating those who wanted to see will quickly translated into action. He criticised the party's lack of enthusiasm in an article in July 1890 in the *Sächsische Arbeiter-Zeitung*, and this effectively inaugurated the conflict.[4]

The other issue had to do with the way the party managed its business. The *Jungen* claimed that it was being run on too authoritarian lines and demanded greater opportunity for the rank-and-file to make its will felt. Heated argument therefore developed around proposals put out by the party in August 1890, the intended effect of which was to strengthen the role of its representatives in parliament. Wille and his friends interpreted this as 'dictatorship' by the parliamentary fraction.

The arguments became increasingly acrimonious, and Wille incautiously let fall a remark about 'corruption' having crept into the party during the period of illegality. Bebel, his aura now greater than ever after seeing the party through its underground phase, felt personally insulted, and made no secret of the fact. The battle was now on, and, as the main spokesman against the *Jungen*, Bebel addressed meetings up and down the country, including a mass rally in Berlin. Wille proved a poor match for so clever and experienced a politician, and Bebel got most of the applause, but the effect of these confrontations on Wille's reputation was dramatic. Hitherto a fairly minor figure in the literary world, he was transformed for the time being into a celebrated personality. He became headline news, with press reports hastening to describe his activity in one town after another, and articles about him appearing in the newspapers. Suddenly he was 'discovered' as far as the general public was concerned.[5]

Then came Georg von Vollmar's two Munich speeches in the summer of 1891, when, as an SPD deputy in the Reichstag, he proclaimed the idea of co-operation between the party and the government. Socialist policies, he believed, could be carried through within the existing state, whereas at the

Berlin meeting Wille had insisted that 'our fraction must be most careful to avoid in any way at all giving the impression that anything can be achieved on the basis of the present social order.[6] This further convinced the *Jungen* that the party was committed to a slow, reformist strategy. The task of winning majority support for their views at the next party congress at Erfurt was pretty hopeless, however, and they suffered total defeat. Werner and Wildberger were expelled from the party, and Wille himself left it at the end of the congress. In November 1891 they and their followers founded their own independent party of Unabhängige Sozialisten, who within a short while had a journal of their own, *Der Sozialist*. We shall follow up what happened then and its very considerable Nietzschean connections and ramifications in a later chapter.

In all this, it must be said, an important part was played by Wille's temperament, above all, his hypersensitive reaction to anything which seemed to infringe his personal autonomy. His lodestar was, and always had been, *Individualität*. It was in order 'to maintain my *Individualität*' that he broke with his family as a youth. When, as a result, 'material adversity subjected me in various ways to proletarian servitude', he learnt 'how even energetic individuals can ... in one way or another be reduced to total slavery'. Already then he was finding pleasure and escape in the literary *bohème*. This he recounts after the affair of the *Jungen* was essentially over,[7] but with it still fresh in his memory, and he now links up his youthful craving for *Individualität* with his experience of what he calls the 'servitude of our time'. This, he comments, was so strong that it came to infect even the party whose aim was emancipation. He had long been moving towards such a point of view and had had to warn himself against getting involved in the 'machinery by which a party makes an individual depend on it'. Political parties seemed to him 'clearly a form of tyranny'. Of whatever kind they were, and whatever their dogma, they embodied 'fanatical intolerance' and 'authoritarianism', and just before the Erfurt congress he turned down the offer of a candidature for the Reichstag on the grounds that all parties were dogmatic and one-sided. He made no secret of his 'contempt for parliamentarism', and the last thing he wanted was to be a 'party man'.[8] This all sounds rather too obviously like second-hand Nietzsche, for whom the party politician was 'inevitably a liar'.[9]

Wille settled at Friedrichshagen, a village in the country near (but not yet part of) Berlin, where he was at an intellectual meeting-point of writers who, while priding themselves on being modern in their approach, had all the same taken refuge from the industrial milieu of the city. Most of the writers there were for socialism, but in the context of a general propensity to radicalism of one kind or another. Thus socialism was often mixed up with anarchism, and each with Nietzsche, and with other things too. 'We look at Nietzsche', one of them said, 'and also to spiritism and theosophy.'[10] The atmosphere could hardly fail to appeal to Wille's romantic egocentricity, and the effect of Nietzsches' influence was to encourage this. Nietzsche was often under discussion at Friedrichshagen, as he was in the Dehmel circle, which Wille frequented. The same applies to the society 'Durch', where also Wille was often to be seen. This was so-called because, as one participant explained, 'we wanted to get "through" to our true selves', that is to say, 'we wanted to develop our own *Individualität*'. Inevitably, he added, Nietzsche found 'enthusiastic advocates' there.[11] There were other members too, like Hermann Bahr, who were strongly drawn to socialism.[12]

Writers other than Nietzsche claimed Wille's attention too; for example, Tolstoi and Ibsen. Ibsen had provided support for the milieu theory of Naturalism, which had been much championed at Friedrichshagen, but the attitude to him began to change. To understand him properly, it was increasingly being said, meant acknowledging the 'rights of *Individualität*', the 'free, limitless living out of *Persönlichkeit*'.[13] It was from this point of view that *An Enemy of the People* was put on by the *Freie Volksbühne* in 1890, and the occasion marked an important episode in the *Jungen* affair.

The Freie Volksbühne had grown out of the example set by the Verein Freie Bühne — the theatre club, not the journal of that name — which had been founded in 1889. It aimed, in association with the Naturalist movement, to facilitate the performance of plays which censorship would not have allowed in the public theatre and to offer drama at cheaper prices to a working-class audience. Wille and others of the *Jungen* were involved in running it, but before long relations between them and representatives of the SPD became strained. Then, in 1892, Wille was replaced as chairman by Franz Mehring.

In the context of the *Jungen* affair, the production of *An Enemy of the People* was from Wille's point of view a calculated act of provocation. As the story of a man who sees through deception and corruption, is vilified by the local population, resolves to educate people to individual freedom and independence of mind, wants to prepare them to recognise the machinations of political leaders, and to show how political parties stifle the thinking of the younger generation, it suited Wille's purposes exactly. In an introductory lecture he went out of his way to publicise the intention behind the production. He was anxious to show that it was directed against the SPD, and he wanted people to identify with its message.[14]

Two years earlier, Wille had written the first of several essays which together furnish a theoretical commentary on the *Jungen* affair. From these one can see very clearly the extent to which Nietzsche had penetrated his thinking, and had been influencing his ideas.

The first of these essays to be considered, 'Der Mensch als Massenmitglied' ('Man as a member of the mass')' published in 1890,[15] dates from the immediate aftermath of Wille's confrontation with Bebel in Berlin. This is the socialist rally referred to in the opening paragraph, 'where the struggle of the "young" and the "old" is being fought out'. It begins by noting with pleasure that recently in Berlin a new catchword has been heard, even on the lips of working-class people, the term — straight from Nietzsche, of course — 'herd animal (*Herdentier*). Wille says that if one worker wants to reproach another with 'mindless docility and acceptance of what you are told', he tells him that he is a 'herd animal in Bruno Wille's sense'. He points out, however, that people tend to contradict themselves. They will support independent attitudes and yet subordinate themselves to a party. The reason is that a person behaves differently in a crowd from how he does as an individual being. For latent in everyone is 'herd nature', and this quality 'becomes particularly effective when man operates in the mass' — Nietzschean doctrine, needless to say, of the most transparent kind.

However, Wille was prepared to recognise positive features in that element in man which makes him happy to be one among many. Without his 'herd nature', he says, man would not be able to develop reason and morality. The individual would be obliterated in the struggle for existence. Being part of a 'faithful mass' may produce bad results, such as religious fanaticism and the burning of witches; but 'mass' strengthens belief, and in politics it can be mainly the size of a party that induces even thinking people to join it. Wille puts the emphasis on the dangers of the effect of mass on man as individual. 'Herd nature' holds back his higher, spiritual life. Under its influence he can become merely an irrational creature, ready to follow the behaviour and thought of others, abandoning 'independence and *Individualitat*'. 'Mass' threatens man's inner freedom, and its overcoming is a major task of humanity. There are too many 'bulwarks of herd nature', pre-eminent among them, from Wille's point of view, the SPD.

The very simplicity of the argument makes it all the more transparently Nietzschean. It culminates, moreover, in praise of solitude as the 'mother of great thoughts', whereas the 'crowd submerges the thoughts and feelings of the individual'. Wille's advice is thus tantamount to Zarathustra's 'flee ... into your solitude',[16] and at the end he slips into Zarathustra's characteristic tone of lyrical exultation. Thus, Zarathustra: 'O solitude, solitude, you are my home! How blissfully and tenderly your voice speaks to me',[17] and Wille:

'O individual, I sing my praise to you! Sufficiency unto oneself (*Selbstherr-lichkeit*)! You are the sublimest crown of all'.

The second of these essays, 'Gemüts-Individualismus' ('Individualism of the mind'),[18] belongs to the phase between the confrontation in Berlin and the Erfurt congress.

Wille notes that people think differently about certain matters and asks why this should be so. Where politics and parties are concerned varying interests play a part, but it is not just considerations of material advantage, Wille says, that move a person to join one party rather than another. Spiritual and cultural factors are also involved, and they are very important. Any one-sidedly materialistic view of life is to be condemned. It assumes that once the socio-economic ideal has been attained all problems are solved. But this is a great over-simplification, and so is socialism if it rests only on this belief.

Truth, Wille goes on to argue, is not as clear-cut as this. It may be commendable to believe that we ought not to let our thinking be influenced by our emotional life, but this is impossible. Our dearest convictions have always been 'built essentially out of our love for what we feel'. This is in line with Nietzsche's warning against the 'clutch of such contradictory ideas as "pure reason", "absolute intellect", "perception in and for itself"',[19] and Wille clearly goes along with Nietzsche's insistence, where logic is concerned, on the need to be sceptical as to its claims and possibilities. He is also turning Nietzsche's 'perspectivism' to account. For, Nietzsche said, to be able to take an objective view of anything requires 'an eye not looking in any direction, one where the active and interpreting forces are neutralised, indeed should be lacking altogether', and this, he insisted, 'cannot possibly be conceived'. There is only 'perspectivistic understanding'. 'The more and the more different eyes', Nietzsche said, 'we are able to bring to bear on the same matter, the more complete will our "idea" of this be, the greater will be our "objectivity"'.[20]

The relevance for Wille of Nietzsche's perspectivism becomes apparent when he applies these considerations to the question of the representation of the people in parliament and thus to one of the main issues involved in the *Jungen* affair. The *Jungen* opposed reliance on parliament on the grounds that this put the many in the hands of the few, but, as Nietzsche was there to point out, everything depends on how you look at it. The leadership, viewing the problem only from one particular angle, could not claim that its answer was the only correct one. Moreover, if people hand over their political welfare to those acting on their behalf, they neglect their own political education. Then they create 'professional politicians, charlatans, demagogues and despots', and allow themselves to be shut up in 'party cages'.

The image of the 'party cage' is revealing and makes all the more obvious the parallel with Nietzsche's notion of man, like a tamed animal, restricted by civilisation and needing to return to the wild to recover strength and instinct.[21] This is to insist on the importance of the will as the driving force in life, and so in the title of the essay *Gemüt* loses its more commonly inward and passive associations. It becomes more akin to 'will' and figures in a way clearly reminiscent of the voluntaristic aspects of Nietzsche's philosophy. 'The individualism of *Gemüt*', Wille says, 'is a powerful driving force in the world of ideas.' 'What one feels' is what 'generates thought'. Man owes his highest ideals to the 'energy of individual feeling'; hence the importance for the *Jungen* of the issue of May Day as a release of spontaneous feeling, and their indignation at the way the leadership failed to respond to the demand for such expression of the popular will.

The third and longest of the three essays, entitled 'Philosophie des reinen Mittels' ('Philosophy of the pure means'), was published in instalments in the *Freie Bühne* during 1892.[22] Post-dating the Erfurt congress, it was an attempt, Wille said, to 'combine personal freedom with socialism'.[23] Ibsen figures in the argument, and Stockman's speech in *An Enemy of the People* is used to demonstrate that 'the majority never has right on its side', that it is 'the mass, the majority, the accursedly compact majority', which 'pollutes the source of our spiritual life and poisons the ground under our feet'. Nietzsche, however, plays a more fundamental part; the essay depends heavily on his voluntaristic doctrines and on his stress on man as individual. Wille's idea of the 'free man of reason (*freier Vernunftmensch*)' is clearly a near-relation of Nietzsche's 'free spirit (*freier Geist*)', and what Wille says about the 'enslavement of the will', and about man being locked up in the 'prison of morality', is too obviously Nietzschean to need elucidation. Wille insists that the individual should be free to determine his own situation through evaluating it 'in his own individual way'. What is 'individual' must not be restrained. All 'domination by the majority' is bad, so too is egalitarianism. It is, moreover, with explicit support from Nietzsche that Wille condemns the materialist view of history. The argument about the individual *versus* the masses leans heavily on Nietzsche's concept of 'higher man' and of the upwards thrust of mankind in its finest representatives, and acknowledgement is duly paid to Nietzsche's 'prophetic call' to go the way from man to Superman. Among the enemies to be overcome, Wille argues now with increasing force, is the state. What he had shown in this essay, he commented later was 'how an omnipresent, all-powerful state ... would hamper the emergence of differences of quality between people and also the development of libertarian ideas, just as the medieval hierarchy did in its time'.[24] The phrase 'socialism without bondage by the state' would sum up what Wille was after. These words come from a slightly later essay, its title ('Vom rothen Götzen') being a near-replica of the title of a section in *Thus spake Zarathustra* in which the state comes under particularly violent attack.

There cannot, in short, be any doubt as to the extent to which Nietzsche coloured the thinking and terminology of these essays. The question now arises as to the importance of the affair to which they were all related.

It was said at the time, from a point of view sympathetic to the *Jungen*, that 'the battle fought out at Erfurt was a class-struggle in which petty-bourgeois socialism finally defeated proletarian socialism'.[25] This is mis-conceived — rather it is Wille's touchy individualism that above all deserves to be described as petty-bourgeois, especially bearing in mind how quickly he later settled for an easier and more acquiescent attitude when all the fuss was over.[26] The *Jungen* affair caused a lot of furore while it was in progress. In the history of the SPD, however, it must rank as little more than an episode. Interesting as it is from the point of view of the reception of Nietz-sche at this stage of the Wilhelmine period, it would have occurred without Nietzsche in the background and would have followed the same course, from its euphoric beginnings to its final failure. The affair changed nothing as far as the party was concerned. Wille's chances of success were clearly minimal. His hazy socialism and contempt for the discipline and obligations of organ-ised politics were no basis for success within a party as highly organised as the SPD and led by men who commanded such loyalty and affection.

In a wider context, however, the affair was of more significance, especially if one recalls that it was an anarchist, Johann Most, who first, in about 1880, launched an attack on the SPD leadership from a radical point of view, prompting Wilhelm Liebknecht to distance himself and his party from Most's views. This was the first occasion in the history of the SPD, it has been pointed out, on which a dividing-line was drawn between the majority of the party and a radical minority.[27] It is a significant precedent, since the key to the broader importance of the *Jungen* affair lies in the interplay, so clearly illustrated in Wille's essays and helped along by Nietzsche, of a romantically individualistic idea of socialism, and a view of the state so scornful as to suggest obvious associations with anarchism.

Indeed, after the defeat of the *Jungen*, a leading socialist newspaper commented that all that now remained to them was 'inner withdrawal' or 'advance to conscious anarchism'.[28] One writer, a convert from the ranks of SPD orthodoxy to the cause of the *Jungen*, spoke of the influence that he expected 'revolutionary anarchism' now to have on the further develop-ment of German Social Democracy,[29] and many years later a prominent anarchist spoke of the interest which anarchistically-minded people had taken in the affair.[30] In this movement, Kurt Eisner said, 'can be detected something that goes beyond socialism'; Nietzsche's influence, that is to say, had turned some supporters of Social Democracy into, as he put it, 'poetic anarchists'.[31] The debate between Marxism and anarchism which began in 1891 amid the growing isolation of the *Jungen*, was settled in favour of anarchism, and it was the conversion of two of the *Jungen*, Werner and Wildberger, that helped to tip the balance. It should be emphasised too that there are very striking parallels between Wille's ideas and those put forward by Benedikt Friedländer, an acknowledged anarchist, in *Der freiheitliche Sozialismus und der Staatsknechttum der Marxisten*, published in 1892 with the affair of the *Jungen* in mind. Friedländer condemned the prevailing socialism from much the same point of view as Wille, and lampooned it, as Nietzsche had done, as despotic and terroristic. Wille was not afraid to point out that Friedländer was a friend of his.[32] Moreover, when the series of *Flugschriften für den individualistischen Anarchismus* began to appear in 1898, it was edited by a man, Bernhard Zack, who had come to anarchism via involvement with the *Jungen*.[33]

The anarchist impulse in the *Jungen* affair markedly increased as their prospects deteriorated. Before Erfurt they had been revolutionary social democrats rather than anarchists. Thereafter they were essentially anarchists first and foremost, and it is not by chance that it was in the last of Wille's relevant essays that his development in this direction was most clearly delineated. It is correct to say that German anarchism, 'which had greatly gained in importance as a result of these events, began to become conscious of itself once more and entered a period of renewed upswing'.[34]

This came about as the anarchist momentum apparent among the *Jungen* transferred itself to the Unabhängige Sozialisten, their natural successors. The mouthpiece of the Unabhängige Sozialisten was *Der Sozialist*. After its switch to anarchism it was edited by Gustav Landauer, who owed even more to Nietzsche, and in a profounder sense, than Wille. So there is more yet to be said about Nietzsche's role in German anarchist thinking, and we shall come to this in due course.

Notes to Chapter I

[1] For a detailed account cf. Dirk H. Muller, *Idealismus und Revolution: zur Opposition der Jungen gegen den Sozialdemokratischen Parteivorstand 1890 bis 1894* (Berlin, 1975). Cf. likewise Herbert Scherer, *Bürgerlich-oppositionelle Literaten und*

sozialdemokratische Arbeitbewegung nach 1890 (Stuttgart, 1974). Also, H. M. Bock, 'Die "Literaten – und Studentenrevolte" in der SPD um 1900', in *Das Argument*, 13 Jg. (1971), pp. 23 ff.

[2]   Letter dated 7 September 1890 to the *Sächische Arbeiter-Zeitung.*

[3]   For relevant details cf. V. L. Little, *The Outlawed Party: Social Democracy in Germany 1878–1890* (Princeton, 1966, pp. 302 ff.

[4]   Cf. Hans Müller, *Werth und Bedeutung politischer Demonstrationen: Festschrift zur Maifeier* (Berlin, 1892).

[5]   Cf. Adolf von Hanstein, *Das jüngste Deutschland* (Leipzig, 1901), p. 188.

[6]   Quoted in Hans Müller, *Der Klassenkampf in der deutschen Sozialdemokratie* (Zurich, 1892), p. 93.

[7]   Cf. *Freie Bühne* (1892), pp. 23–4.

[8]   *Aus Traum und Kampf* 3rd ed., (Berlin, 1920), p. 26.

[9]   *Werke*, II, p. 1222.

[10]   Hanstein, *op. cit.*, p. 29.

[11]   *Ibid.*, p. 79.

[12]   Cf. Little, *op. cit.*, p. 307.

[13]   Max Halbe, 'Berliner Brief', in *Die Gesellschaft* (1889), pp. 1171 ff.

[14]   Cf. Wille's article 'Die Freie Volksbühne und der Polizei-Präsident', in *Freie Bühne* (1891), pp. 673 ff.

[15]   *Ibid.*, (1890), pp. 865 ff.

[16]   *Werke*, II, p. 316.

[17]   *Ibid.*, p. 433.

[18]   *Freie Bühne* (1891), pp. 305 ff.

[19]   *Werke*, II, p. 860.

[20]   *Ibid.*, II, p. 861.

[21]   Cf. *ibid.*, II, pp. 979–80. Cf. T. J. Reed, 'Nietzsche's animals: idea, image and influence', in Malcolm Pasley (ed.), *Nietzsche, Imagery and Thought* (London, 1978).

[22]   Then, in extended form as a book, *Philosophie der Befreiung durch das reine Mittel: Beiträge zur Pädagogik des Menschengeschlechtes* (Berlin, 1894).

[23]   'Vom rothen Götzen', in *Die Zukunft* (1894), p. 458 n.

[24]   'Schattenbilder vom Zukunftsstaate', in *Neue deutsche Rundschau/Freie Bühne* (1894), p. 1040.

[25]   Hans Müller, *Der Klassenkampf in der deutschen Sozialdemokratie*, p. 116.

[26]   Cf. pp. 56–7.

[27]   Cf. H. M. Bock, *Syndikalismus und Linkskommunismus von 1918–1923* (Meisenheim am Glau, 1969), p. 6.

[28]   *Die Neue Zeit* (1891–2), p. 165.

[29]   Anon., *Die Hintermänner der Sozialdemokratie* (Berlin, 1890), p. 4.

[30]   Cf. Rudolf Rocker, *Aus den Memoiren eines deutschen Anarchisten* (Frankfurt am Main, 1974), pp. 37 ff.

[31]   *Psychopathia spiritualis*, p. 87. Cf. Chapter II, note 9.

[32]   Cf. 'Selbstporträt', in *Die Gesellschaft* (1893), p. 169.

[33]   Cf. Ulrich Linse, *Organisierter Anarchismus im deutschen Kaiserreich* (Wiesbaden, 1969), p. 81.

[34]   The remark occurs in the penultimate (unsigned) article on anarchism in *Die Kritik* (28 September 1895).

II

Social Democracy, ideology, and Nietzsche

The charge levelled by the *Jungen* against the officialdom of the SPD was essentially that it allowed too little scope to feeling and the imagination. The way literature was sometimes talked about in party circles might support this, and two articles in *Die Neue Zeit*, written when the *Jungen* affair was at its height, illustrate the problem. One was by Wilhelm Liebknecht. Together with Bebel, he had been one of the founders of the party, a man with a long history of political struggle behind him since his days of exile in Switzerland and London. The other was by the socialist writer Robert Schweichel.

Liebknecht was convinced that contemporary writers hardly knew what social problems were about. If the sum total of your knowledge of the present day, he said, was what you got from their plays, you would have learnt next to nothing, and that, he thought, was all the writers themselves knew about it. He went out of his way to say that, in any case, literature does not matter, 'Germany engaged in political struggle has no time for poetry'. For Schweichel too contemporary literature was bourgeois, irrelevant and morally confused.

These statements provoked the retort from one leading writer that, while Social Democracy might talk a lot about revolutionary change, it could be as stuck-in-the-mud as any conservative. Schweichel might complain that the new literature lacked a firm moral standpoint, but this only showed to what an extent even a man like himself was hidebound by tradition. The way he spoke about literature and morals reminded one, it was said, of nothing so much as the indignation you might expect from a priest discovering that socialism preached free love.[1] Otto Brahm, a founder of the Freie Bühne and later director of the Deutsches Theater in Berlin, likewise called Liebknecht to account for his reactionary and paternalistic attitude.[2]

Brahm concerns us also as the man whom Franz Mehring attacked in one of his most important statements about Nietzsche. After studying classics at Leipzig and Berlin, Mehring had been active as a journalist in the liberal cause and then in 1891 had joined the SPD, quickly becoming one of its most dogmatic and influential ideologists. The comments in question about Nietzsche formed part of his *Kapital und Presse* of 1891. Basically, the reason for his antipathy to Brahm, and for his desire to discredit him was that Brahm had, unsuccessfully, taken him to court for allegedly insulting him in what he had written under the title *Der Fall Lindau.*[3] Mehring associated Brahm with Lindau, a writer whose reputation rested mainly on a number of popular dramas, on the grounds that the Naturalists, for all their socialist sympathies, were as much champions of capitalism as Lindau himself. Together, Mehring said, Brahm and Lindau formed a 'closed ring'.[4] One section of *Kapital und Presse* ('On the philosophy and literature of capitalism'), contains attacks both on Brahm and Lindau, and couples Brahm with Nietzsche with a view to discrediting him too. All three figure in the opening paragraph. 'Now it only remains', Mehring writes, 'to destroy the banner beneath which the Lindau ring has fought its glorious battle – the banner on which Herr Otto Brahm's hand has so cleverly written "Beyond Good and Evil" ...'.[5]

The central point of Mehring's attack on Nietzsche is Lindau's description of Nietzsche as the 'social philosopher of socialism'. Mehring denies that he could be so described. On the contrary, he says, Nietzsche was the 'social philosopher of capitalism'. He then sketches the historical and philosophical development to show how Nietzsche came about. It was not the bourgeoisie but the working class that succeeded in maintaining links with the classical tradition of German culture, and it was Lassalle, Engels and Marx who recognised its revolutionary value. Conservative opinion, however, was unable to follow in that direction, so that after the failure and disillusion of 1848 it rejected Hegel and adopted Schopenhauer, the 'philosopher of a moneyed and philistine bourgeoisie that wanted nothing more than peace and quiet'.[6] Nietzsche, Mehring points out, admired Schopenhauer for a while, but then, as times changed, he 'placed his laurel wreath no longer on the class of moneyed leisure, but on exploitation and high finance'.[7] He treated progressive movements in history with scorn, did not recognise the historically determined nature of morality, and so came to reject morality altogether. Thus, says Mehring, he could regard envy, hatred, greed and lust for power as desirable for the furtherance of 'life'. Moreover, he regarded the class struggle not as a dialectical process, but as 'master-morality' versus 'slave-morality', as a struggle in which the 'rulers and oppressors, the "free spirits", always have power, and hence right, on their side, whereas the ruled and oppressed, the *Herdenvieh*, are for ever condemned to impotence and to being in the wrong'.[8] There follows a long quotation from *Beyond Good and Evil*, the point of which is to show how Nietzsche here expounds the philosophy of capitalism. For Mehring Nietzsche was thus no problem at all. There was nothing to be said in his favour, and all socialists had to do was to ignore him.

It was very different in the case of Kurt Eisner, nearly a generation younger than Mehring, and only twenty-four when he published his long essay on Nietzsche entitled *Psychopathia spiritualis*,[9] dated the same year as *Kapital und Presse*, and in part a reply to it. The son of a Berlin manufacturer, Eisner was from 1896 till his dismissal in 1905 an editor of *Vorwärts*, and from 1910 a free-lance writer in Munich. He became an outspoken opponent of the war and thereafter, till his murder, head of the short-lived Bavarian Republic.

Eisner explains in the *Psychopathia spiritualis* that he had been thinking about Nietzsche for some time before knowing anything of his work — illustrating the fact that, with Nietzsche so much in the air, one did not need to have studied him to fall under his spell. Merely what he had read about him, Eisner said, was sufficient to obsess him to an uncanny extent. By the time he wrote the *Psychopathia spiritualis*, he said, he viewed Nietzsche, if not as a model to be followed, at any rate as a gripping phenomenon and a great temptation; hence his intention now to take a critical look at the nature and implications of his thought. Thus, when a few years later his wife became a Nietzsche enthusiast, he was in a position to point out to her the risks involved, and to warn her, in the light of his own experience, against the dangers.[10] Nietzsche, he told her, was one of the greatest poets, one of the most refined of people, with one of the cleverest minds. But he was not a philosopher by any stretch of the imagination. Behind the allures of a profound thinker 'is concealed a monster of a thinker', and much that he says shows lack of understanding, even ignorance. His advice to her was to keep off Nietzsche, reiterating the quotation from *Thus spake Zarathustra* with which he had opened the *Psychopathia spiritualis*: 'Verily, my advice is this: go away from me and protect yourself against Zarathustra! And better still, be ashamed of him! It may be that he deceived you'.

In this work Eisner states the case against Nietzsche from the point of view of a socialist anxious to ward off the erosion of his own socialist convictions, and, as he well knew, his own beliefs were not in all respects as firm as they might have been. This applied notably in the matter of historical materialism. His lack of conviction on this central aspect of Marxist doctrine — it is no more, he says, than a 'half truth' — is one reason why he found Nietzsche so attractive in the first place.[11] If he had had no doubts on this score, he would, we may safely assume, have been immune to Nietzsche to start with. However, the fact that Eisner's socialism was less dogmatically assured than Mehring's helped to make his interpretation of Nietzsche more sensitive and understanding.

As the *Psychopathia spiritualis* is a step in Eisner's self-liberation from Nietzsche, he tends to be most severe about those aspects of Nietzsche which earlier he had found most appealing. It is the romantic side of Nietzsche that he now particularly condemns: 'Romantic is the oracular element ... Romantic is his catchword about the emancipation of the flesh ... Romantic is the way he mixes up art and scholarship'.[12] At the same time, he goes some way towards identifying himself with views of Nietzsche which help to explain the side of him he is criticising. He is notably sympathetic to Nietzsche's revulsion against features in society springing, as Eisner puts it with clearly affirmative implications, 'from all this boring and barren lack of ideas, from all this mediocrity that levels everything down, from all this empty and opportunistic utilitarianism ...'[13] Eisner thus implicitly sides with Nietzsche's idea of the need for people above the common average, and shares his scorn for the drab reduction of everyone and everything to a low denominator. However, as he says in his discussion of the question of Nietzsche and socialism, the greatest minds do not necessarily make the most fruitful contribution to the development of mankind, and socialism is poorly served by romantic kinds of argument, however brilliant they may be. It calls for 'clear heads', and it is a practical goal. But 'in Nietzscheanism I sleepwalk in search of a blue flower, suggested to me as in a dream'.[14]

So, Eisner's essay vacillates between tributes to Nietzsche and criticism of him. There is enough of the one to make it perhaps surprising that there is so much of the other. The reason is that in writing this essay he is fighting the temptations that Nietzsche put in his way; hence the stress on Nietzsche's romanticism in the early part of the essay, hence too his emphasis, as if to convince himself, on the finality of Nietzsche's failure. Nietzsche's star, he says, 'will burn itself out', 'the future does not belong to Nietzsche', and 'simple minded socialism will march forward'.[15] Rigid and dogmatic in his thinking, Mehring had done his best to discredit Nietzsche wholly and absolutely, as a menace to the ideology he himself represented. If Mehring was cast in an ideological mould, Eisner was certainly not, and in writing about Nietzsche he had a double incentive — in protest against Mehring, to stress his merits, and, in his own interests, to identify his dangers.

Nothing, Eisner says, would have displeased Nietzsche more, and justifiably so, than to be labelled the philosopher of capitalism. He was an 'aristocrat of the spirit', and would have been a thousand times more disposed to defend the 'feudalism of the family tree' than that 'of the money-safe'.[16] It seemed to Mehring, according to Eisner, that with the advent of Nietzsche — of a philosophy, that is to say, whose material basis in capitalism was to him so obvious — historical materialism proved itself right yet again; and, we might add, it was because Mehring was so cocksure about historical materialism that the equation of Nietzsche and capitalism was to him so self-evident.

A figure such as Nietzsche had to be shown to be one with the major material factor of the age, if historical materialism was always and inevitably right. Eisner was less certain about this. So, when he attacks Mehring's conclusions, he falls back, in Nietzsche's defence, on features which elsewhere in his essay he criticises as among Nietzsche's weaknesses, as merely 'romantic'. He says that Nietzsche was in no way 'bogged down', as Mehring liked to think, in the ordinary world. His philosophy can only breathe in ethereal heights, and it disregards the conditions of real life. Nietzsche is a dreamer, and his dreams do not originate in the material world. The reason why Mehring is so keen to interpret Nietzsche's dreams by reference to capitalism is because he himself is so obsessed with it. It is not Nietzsche, the dreamer, but Mehring, the interpreter of dreams who bears witness to the idea of historical materialism. Nietzsche's dream is of a golden age of human perfection, and for him the aristocratic principle is all-important. But, Eisner goes on, if for one single moment he had awoken from his dreams and observed how this works in real life, he would have discovered to his horror that the only 'aristocratic' force is that of money. Nietzsche, in fact, 'completely overlooked capitalism', and Eisner finds it revolting to see him portrayed as the 'door-keeper of Bleichröder or Rothschild'. He was at most the philosopher of unconscious capitalism, and even then, he says, he 'opposes and contradicts himself'.

Eisner was certainly on the right lines as regards Nietzsche and capitalism, if only because Mehring's view made Nietzsche the direct embodiment of a dimension of life, economics and politics, which he so despised. It was the negation of the 'artistic culture' which became for him of paramount importance, despite his earlier interest in political events. 'Culture and the state', he said, are 'antagonisms', and great periods of culture were for him periods of decline as far as politics are concerned.[17] His sympathy came to be entirely with people who set themselves high and distant objectives; his preferred option was 'isolation'. Above all, he admired 'independent minds (*Freigesinnte*)', who live only for the task of 'understanding (*Erkenntnis*)', and keep their sense of contact with society so tenuous 'that a great transformation of outward things, even an upheaval in the political order, does not at the same time disorientate their own life'.[18] True, Nietzsche had been once desperately worried about the threat of just such a change. The possibility of proletarian revolution had greatly occupied him at the time of the Paris Commune, and he had been afraid that it might undermine his personal existence and all he stood for – he soon bothered himself much less about political matters of that sort.

There is other evidence too that endangers Mehring's crude and simple theory — such as, for example, the passage entitled 'The impossible class',[19] about the importance of being 'master over oneself' and the difficulties facing the working class in this regard. This may sound like a purely political statement, an attack on socialism. Socialism however is just one model — a metaphor almost — of the oppression of the individual through forces hindering the realisation of selfhood. The point here about the 'pied pipers of socialism' — socialist leaders and agitators, that is to say — is that, like the wretched material situation in which the workers find themselves, they make it even more difficult for them to be themselves. Or one can take another passage in which Nietzsche says that what rules in the industrial world is the law of adversity; one wants to live, but one has to sell oneself. That too would be an odd defence of capitalism, unless the implication were — which it is not — that this is as it should be.

Mehring too easily bypassed complicating evidence of this sort. He made the mistake too, on the basis of Nietzsche's division of people into 'masters' and 'slaves' (which suited his argument very well), of assuming that for Nietzsche *Pöbel* ('mob') meant, in a more or less sociological sense, the lower classes. Its essential association, however, is with human quality, or the lack of it, without exclusive reference necessarily to any one section of society. There is 'mob at the top (*Pöbel oben*)' and 'mob at the bottom (*Pöbel unten*)',[20] and there is an 'educated, middle-class mob (*gebildeter Pöbel*)', characterised by false and pretentious attitudes, by 'aspirations towards what is sublime and elevated'.[21] It is much the same with *Herde*, an image above all of mediocrity wherever it is to be found. So Nietzsche talks of the 'herd animal with its profound mediocrity, its fears, and the way it gets bored with itself'.[22] He calls it a 'diminished, almost ridiculous sort of creature, well-meaning, ailing, and mediocre'.[23] The contrast with 'herd animals' is provided by people who are able to become more than mediocre, to manifest the qualities of refinement and excellence that Nietzsche subsumes under the concept of *Vornehmheit*. These qualities are attainable by people 'able to shape themselves, as an artist shapes his material', people capable of 'sublime self-mastery'.[24]

The better some meet this challenge, the more marked, Nietzsche asserts, will be the divergence of order and quality between one person and another. The process by which the weaker are thus marked out is the same as that by which others are enabled to succeed as people, and Nietzsche may well not have excluded the worker as eligible, like everyone else, to qualify for his 'aristocratic' world.[25] The workers, he stated, 'are one day to live as the bourgeois do today, but being superior to them — the higher caste; thus poorer and simpler, but in possession of power'.[26] 'Higher caste' does not mean socially determined class, and in any case what Nietzsche is talking about is not present reality, but future prospect. Nietzsche's idea of *Masse* fits into this general context. It is not just a synonym for those on the bottom rungs of the social ladder in the capitalist system. It signifies essentially accumulated and collective mediocrity. A 'declaration of higher men against the mass'[27] means nothing so simple as breaking the power of the proletariat. What has to be fought against is the downward pull of mediocrity — *Masse*, after all, can imply the force of weight as well as of numbers.

However, as a guardian of Marxist orthodoxy, resolved to prove historical materialism right in all particulars and at all costs, Mehring was not likely to spoil his case against Nietzsche by too many ifs and buts. He was nothing if not an ideologist and it is significant that in his short review of Eisner's *Psychopathia spiritualis*[28] he was as much concerned with Eisner's ideological shortcomings as with Nietzsche. Here he was as rigid and dogmatic as he had been in *Kapital und Presse*, and he was so too when he returned to the question of Nietzsche in the final section of *Die Lessing-Legende* which, having appeared in instalments from late January 1892 in *Die Neue Zeit*, was published as a book in 1893. As before, Nietzsche figures as the 'philosopher of *Grosskapital*',[29] and his outstanding people (Superman, 'free spirits', *vornehme Seelen*) are all 'given to exploitation' — capitalists, in fact. As to why Nietzsche went mad, he says that he experienced the 'unbounded horror' created by capitalism, struggled to discover its rationality, and lost his reason in the process.[30]

There was no change in Eisner's case either when very soon afterwards he took up the issue of Nietzsche again in an essay 'Aus dem Nachlass eines Lebenden', dating from 1892 and later included in *Taggeist*.[31] As before, he finds much to criticise in Nietzsche — his denigration of the 'mass of the all-too-many', for instance, and his failure to recognise how 'individual weakness can coalesce to constitute powerful community'. But here too his criticism is tempered with respect. Nietzsche, he says, was a 'diagnostician of genius', one of the most subtle minds of our time', a man to be approached with veneration. One can with complete sincerity and great affection, he says, devote oneself to the fullness and depth of his ideas. But one must do so without slavishly capitulating to him. We must temper our convictions with tolerance and, he adds with a reproving glance in Mehring's direction, we must not be arrogant. We must cease judging Nietzsche from any one particular point of view. Merit belongs to those who create new ideas, and loving your neighbour, he remarks, applies particularly in intellectual life.

Mehring's undifferentiated view of Nietzsche was to exercise enormous influence. It was a major factor in holding back the understanding of Nietzsche in Marxist quarters in Wilhelmine Germany, and it remained decisive for years to come. The idea that all has been said once Nietzsche has been classified as the philosopher of capitalism was too valuable an asset ever to stand much chance of radical revision, given a social and political theory which increasingly insisted on a simple correlation between capitalism and fascism. A more equivocal view of Nietzsche, with greater awareness of inconsistency and contradiction, would have been a far less useful ideological weapon. The outcome, further influenced in due course by the Nietzsche-idolatry of the Nazis, was to make Nietzsche taboo in the communist part of Germany, where the debt to Mehring's interpretation is constantly and reverentially reiterated.[32]

For his part, Eisner too had decided that Nietzsche had to be resisted. Yet Nietzsche remained for him someone from whom one could and had to learn. This was especially so as regards the 'necessity of the individualistic principle',[33] to which Eisner himself was strongly drawn. 'The development of the individual to the complete concentration of all his powers and gifts', he said, was 'the task of mankind.'[34] What he opposed however – and criticised Nietzsche for encouraging – was the 'megalomania of ego-centricity',[35] in the light of which individualism too easily appears as the right of the stronger.[36] Nietzsche's individualism, Eisner rightly said, took him beyond socialism, but for Eisner the individualist principle was one of which socialism needed to be reminded. If, as Eisner insisted, Nietzsche could be regarded by socialists as a 'teacher', it was not least from this point of view. To use him in this way, however, meant overcoming the 'crude dichotomy' of 'aristocracy' and 'democracy'[37] – but without invalidating the aristocratic idea. 'To develop all the seeds of one's selfhood, but in the service of the whole, is the way to true aristocracy.'[38] Therefore, combining Nietzsche's aristocratic principle, his demand for selfhood, and his own socialist ideal, Eisner says 'let the masses be made aristocratic'.[39] One question asked at the time, with Nietzsche in mind, was whether, with the coming of socialism, there would be any place for the 'highest thing that man possesses, for thorough-going subjectivity'.[40] Eisner's answer would have been to say that that was going too far – but he would have very much sympathised with the reasons for asking the question. Mehring's reaction would have been to throw up his hands in horror.

Eisner's wish, therefore, as far as socialism is concerned, was to keep Nietzsche in the picture, Mehring's to keep him out. For socialists, in Mehring's view, he was no help in any possible respect. He was not friend but foe, the mouthpiece of the class enemy. So keen, in fact, was Mehring to dispose of Nietzsche that he could even deny his role in the *Jungen* affair.[41]

Eisner saw the connection clearly enough, critical though he was of the *Jungen* as 'play-actors of their egos', with the crazy notion that, once material difficulties were overcome, the way would be open to the 'development of free, boundless individualism'.[42]

When, a decade and a half later, Eisner was dismissed from his editorial job on *Vorwärts*, it was ostensibly on a charge of revisionism — which he vigorously denied, though the description of him as a 'revisionist with the tactics of a revolutionary has something to be said for it.[43] Nietzsche played an important part in the revisionist movement too. It attracted above all socialists who — like Eisner himself — were critical of historical materialism and its deterministic associations as impersonal, rigid and doctrinaire. From that point of view Nietzsche had for some people in it a natural appeal, and he was an obvious target in the fight against revisionism. How this worked out we shall consider in the following chapter.

Notes to Chapter II

[1] Julius Hart, 'Ein sozialdemokratischer Angriff auf das "jüngste De**n**tschland"', in *Freie Bühne* (1891), pp. 913 ff.

[2] 'Naturalismus und Sozialismus', in *ibid.*, pp. 241 ff.

[3] For accounts of the relevant circumstances, cf. Scherer, *op. cit.*, pp. 121 ff, and Walter Kaufmann, *Franz Mehring: Vertreter des historischen Materialismus* (Wiesbaden, 1966), pp. 36 ff.

[4] *Kapital und Presse*, p. 133.

[5] *Ibid.*, p. 119.

[6] *Ibid.*, p. 120.

[7] *Ibid.*, p. 120.

[8] *Ibid.*, p. 123.

[9] First published in instalments in *Die Gesellschaft* in 1891 under the title 'Friedrich Nietzsche und die Apostel der Zukunft: Beiträge zur moderne Psychopathia spiritualis', and then in book form with title and sub-title reversed: *Psychopathia spiritualis: Friedrich Nietzsche und die Apostel der Zukunft.* (Leipzig, n.d.). References are to the latter. It embraced, it has been said, '*in nuce* his political conception of socialism'; Freya Eisner, *Kurt Eisner: Die Politik des libertären Sozialismus* (Frankfurt am Main, 1979), p. 8.

[10] In a letter of 1898, quoted in Franz Schade, *Kurt Eisner und die bayerische Sozialdemokratie* (Hannover, 1961), p. 27.

[11] *Op. cit.*, p. 94.

[12] *Ibid.*, p. 10.

[13] *Ibid.*, p. 11.

[14] *Ibid.*, p. 86.

[15] *Ibid.*, p. 16.

[16] *Ibid.*, p. 93.

[17] *Werke*, II, p. 985.
[18] *Ibid.*, I, p. 622.
[19] *Ibid.*, I, pp. 1155−7.
[20] *Ibid.*, II, p. 508.
[21] *Ibid.*, II, p. 14.
[22] *Ibid.*, II, p. 218.
[23] *Ibid.*, II, p. 624.
[24] *Ibid.*, II, p. 624.
[25] Cf. Klemens von Klemperer, *Konservative Bewegungen: zwischen Kaiserreich und Nationalsozialismus* (Munich and Vienna, n.d.), p. 67 n.
[26] *Werke*, III, p. 843.
[27] *Ibid.*, p. 430.
[28] *Die Neue Zeit*, 10 Jg. (1891−2), pp. 617−18.
[29] 3rd edition, (Stuttgart, 1909), p. 423.
[30] *Ibid.*, p. 424.
[31] Berlin, 1901.
[32] Cf. for example, Thomas Höhle, *Franz Mehring: Sein Weg zum Marxismus 1869−1891* (Berlin, 1956), p. 281.
[33] *Psychopathia spiritualis*, p. 88.
[34] *Ibid.*, p. 76.
[35] *Ibid.*, p. 76.
[36] *Ibid.*, p. 77.
[37] *Ibid.*, p. 79.
[38] *Ibid.*, p. 79.
[39] *Ibid.*, p. 79.
[40] Franz Servaes, 'Nietzsche und der Sozialismus', in *Freie Bühne*, 3 Jg. (1892), p. 85.
[41] *Die Neue Zeit*, 10 Jg. (1891−2), p. 668.
[42] *Psychopathia spiritualis*, p. 87.
[43] Fritz Oertner in his tribute on Eisner's death, in *Der Syndikalist*, 1 Jg. no. 12 (1 January 1919).

III

Social Democracy, revisionism, and Nietzsche

In the last chapter we noted features in Eisner's general attitude which were open to criticism from a rigidly doctrinaire point of view like Mehring's. We observed too, by comparison with Mehring, Eisner's more open-minded approach to Nietzsche. At the same time, we detected a connection between these two aspects. Thus, we can more easily appreciate the fact that when a revisionist movement came to the fore within German socialism Nietzsche played an important part in the debate.

It was Eduard Bernstein, a German exile living in London, who brought the issue of revisionism to a head in articles in *Die Neue Zeit* in 1895 and 1896. Then, shortly after his return to Germany, he developed the argument in his book *Die Voraussetzungen des Sozialismus und die Aufgabe der Sozial-demokratie* (1899). New movements always tend to look around for thinkers who might be useful as allies, and it was not long before Nietzsche was being talked about in revisionist circles.

The leading revisionist journal was the *Sozialistische Monatshefte*. Originally known as *Der sozialistische Akademiker*, it was founded by Josef Bloch, who edited it until its suppression in 1933. It adopted a position at the opposite extreme to that of party spokesmen who held that political struggle made the arts irrelevant, and it inclined towards a more individualistic philosophy than was compatible with the extremes of Marxist materialism and historical determinism. Impatience with the demands of both was a major motivating factor in the revisionist philosophy. Among its preoccupations was the problem of how to combine the claims of the individual with the requirements of socialism. Bloch's idea of socialism was of a complex of feelings ultimately justified in terms of the personality of individuals, and this attitude went hand in hand with a steady interest in Nietzsche. In an article under the pseudonym Catilina, on Bismarck's eightieth birthday in 1895, in *Der sozialistische Akademiker*, he showed himself well aware of the ambivalent use which could be made of Nietzsche's writings, but remained a lifelong admirer of his work.[1]

As one might expect, therefore, articles on Nietzsche figured from time to time in the *Sozialistische Monatshefte*. The first was in 1897 by Hermann Duncker entitled 'Eine Philosophie für das Proletariat' ('A philosophy for the proletariat').[2] This was mainly concerned with recommending the ideas of

Max Stirner to socialists, and urging them not to be put off by his associations with anarchism. Duncker reflects on the significance for socialists of philosophy directed towards the individual (*Ich-Philosophie, Individualphilosophie*), which has 'found its most recent and most brilliant representative in Friedrich Nietzsche'. The 'uncompromising way in which it concentrates on a person's inmost self-awareness' makes it 'particularly apt for the worker', the idea being that the worker's 'sense of *Persönlichkeit*' is heightened by his having to sell himself on the market. Stirner's book 'should therefore be in every worker's hand'. Chronologically, of course, Nietzsche post-dates Stirner, but Duncker reverses the sequence. For him Stirner merely completed what Nietzsche had begun.

Then, when Nietzsche's death in 1900 gave rise to obituaries and articles about him in a number of journals, the *Sozialistische Monatshefte* joined in with an essay arguing the relevance of Nietzsche from its own point of view.[3] The author was Ernst Gystrow (alias Willy Hellpach), and its title promised 'something about Nietzsche and us socialists'.

Previous articles by Gystrow help to elucidate his general position. One, published in 1896, reflects his interest in aesthetics,[4] another, three years later, in the importance of 'psychological' factors in the causality of historical development.[5] Then, in an article written in the same year as the Nietzsche essay,[6] he emphasised the supreme significance of 'genius' and the difficulty of accounting for it in materialist terms. The counter-figure is Mehring, whose alleged ignorance on such matters Gystrow attacks in the second of these contributions.

It is to Mehring, moreover, that he refers in his article on Nietzsche. Anyone, he says, who did not know Nietzsche through his writings, but only from the image of him presented in those 'odd interpretations' popular a little while ago, would not expect him to be of any interest now. If he was as bad as that, he would surely by now be buried and forgotten. For were we not told that he was the 'philosopher of the bourgeoisie', the 'virtuoso who dressed up the brutal practices of the industrial barons and the oligarchs of the commercial world in the glittering garments of ethics', the man who hated socialism and christianity alike 'because both stand in opposition to the worship of the golden calf'? If that's your view, says Gystrow, there is nothing more to say. However, the 'Marxist cliché' is not the last word. We have only to look beyond a narrow view of Nietzsche as the 'philosopher of capitalism' to find that he is very much alive and very important. He was not the 'philosopher of capitalism' nor was he the 'philosopher of romanticism' (a reference presumably to Eisner). He was, socialists should recognise, 'one of us'.

The socialism of which Gystrow claims Nietzsche as an ally rested on assumptions very different from those of the Marxists. It challenged the doctrine of historical materialism and the limitations which its determinism set on the role of the individual in history. Also, it meant discarding belief in any 'final crisis' of capitalism as in the nature of things and therefore in an inevitable revolution ushering in socialism. With the advent of revisionism, Gystrow therefore argues, socialism has substituted 'an ideal that does not lie in the future, but one which it carries in itself', and this is 'close to that to which Nietzsche directed mankind'. These are provocative words, after all that had been said against Nietzsche by so powerful an authority in the SPD as Mehring. Mehring clearly thought that he had disposed of Nietzsche as far as the party was concerned. That did not now seem to be the case.

Gystrow goes on in his article to define socialism above all in economic terms — oddly, it might seem, bearing in mind Nietzsche's antipathy to that side of life. He says that the 'socialist ideal is economic democratisation' which he contrasts with 'political democratisation'. Political democracy has its value, and what socialism stands to gain from it is not to be despised. But it is not specifically socialist, nor is it a condition of the development of socialism. Gystrow makes a lot of this distinction, and we may well wonder why. In fact, as we discover, Nietzsche is behind it.

The argument goes like this. Political democracy is a way of 'leading the masses', and it involves a certain 'accommodation to the instincts of the masses'. The Nietzschean associations of this idea are echoed in the ensuing comment that 'aristocratic minds' will not find this an attractive picture. Political democracy, we are reminded, earned Nietzsche's scorn and contempt. Economic democracy is a very different matter. It cannot just be 'introduced', as political democracy was in Germany; it is utopian to imagine that it could be. It cannot be established without changes in the mode of production, and these can only come about gradually. Also, political democracy is relatively easy to manage, and mistakes do not necessarily lead to disaster. But in the economic sphere they can mean catastrophe. Also, Gystrow argues that the workers are not yet in a position to govern. Only the 'courtiers of the proletariat' — the 'unfortunately all-too-many', in Gystrow's give-away phrase — can persuade them that they can.

The echo of Nietzsche's *Vielzuviele* focuses the discussion on Nietzsche, and what follows makes his significance for Gystrow even more apparent. It took a long time, he notes, for the bourgeoisie to be able to take command of the economy. It will take the working class a long time too. It was a long process, but for this reason one with crucial consequences for the bourgeoisie and its character as a class. That is to say, it was as a result of the protracted period during which it came to acquire economic supremacy that the bourgeoisie, once a homogeneous class, became a more differentiated one. Given time, the same can happen with the proletariat. Then it will lose its characteristics as a solid mass at the bottom of society.

Nietzsche applied the principle of differentiation to people in general; some are better fitted to make something of themselves than others. Gystrow adapts the principle to the working class. He had said that economic democracy takes a long time. This is one of its special advantages from his point of view, and it is for this reason that it can become the basis for the 'spiritual aristocratisation of the masses'. What Bernstein prophesied is bound to happen: proletariat ceases to be a 'uniform concept'. Elaborating this, Gystrow speaks loud and clear the language of Nietzschean individualism. Only through economic democracy within the proletariat is an 'unfolding of spiritual and moral *Individualität*, imaginable. This, and this alone, would make an 'awakening of the feeling of selfhood' possible. He points out that this had long been a prominent feature of bourgeois culture. Its force must now come to be felt in the working class, despite the stress on materialism and determinism in the ideology created on its behalf. 'When this feeling of selfhood', he writes, 'comes with elemental power to permeate the layers of society which have most sharply denied it, their eyes will turn to Friedrich Nietzsche.'

Socialists, Gystrow therefore insists, can now regard Nietzsche, philosopher of the 'aristocratic principle', as 'our prophet'. Nietzsche himself did not realise this, nor have we as yet. He hated socialism and did not understand it. But so long as the dictatorship of the proletariat was insisted on he could have no inkling, in the world of socialism, of differentiation of and within *Persönlichkeit*. Of course, a major gulf dividing socialists from Nietzsche had been Nietzsche's insistence on the supremacy of some and the inferiority of others, of 'masters' and 'slaves'. Here now was a theory which, building on Nietzsche and providing for the process of differentiation to operate within the proletariat, capitalised the aristocratic principle in the interests of the working class. Nietzsche held that the elite of 'higher men' would be the law-givers of the future, and Gystrow's theory allowed the working class to qualify for that role. The key was differentiation; the more the working class participated in economic democracy, the more likely it was that differentiation would come about, and the greater in the long run would be the part played by the working class in government and society.

Moreover, it was not long before, in another contribution to the *Sozialistische Monatshefte*, a revisionist argument was again associated with the name of Nietzsche.[7] The article admitted that the liberation of the working class could only be brought about by the working class itself. But this did not mean that the mass of the proletariat was 'specifically the pathfinder of socialism' or 'the best judge in every issue in matters of politics and society'. To imagine it was was a great mistake and talk of a class-conscious proletariat, such as socialist agitators indulged in, was 'poisonous' propaganda. In any case, the mass of the proletariat, whether Social Democrat or not, was as little class-conscious in any clear and theoretical sense as any other class and as little able 'critically to think through new ideas or to have a well founded judgment about complicated issues of economic life'; hence the emphasis in this article on the 'importance of outstanding minorities' in the socialist movement. One must recognise, it said, how absurd it is to regard the 'conscious stress on able individual minds' as an offence against the principle of democracy, as derogation of the masses. There are obvious parallels here with Gystrow's emphasis on the need to encourage, as against the levelling pressure of the ideal of solidarity, diversification of quality and ability within the working class. Much is made, therefore, of the argument in Ibsen's *An Enemy of the People* against the claims of the 'compact majority', and a reference to *Brand* serves to highlight the importance Ibsen attached to the 'unconditional assertion of *Persönlichkeit* in the cause of an individual ideal'. Freedom and truth call for 'self-affirmation (*Selbstbehauptung*)', and this is where Nietzsche comes in. The motto of his work, it is stated, could be 'be yourself' and, even more radically than Ibsen, he took his stand on the 'absolute right of *Persönlichkeit*'. With Ibsen and Nietzsche is linked Max Stirner, with his attempt to establish the 'self-justification (*Selbstherrlichkeit*) of the individual as a political principle'.

The role played by Nietzsche in the *Sozialistische Monatshefte* is all the more noteworthy since at around the same time he was coming to the fore elsewhere in the revisionist movement, in the journal *Die Neue Gesellschaft*.

This journal was closely bound up with the political careers of two notable members of the SPD, Heinrich and Lily Braun, in the period preceding and following the Dresden party congress of 1903, and they launched it when, with trouble brewing, they wanted to be sure of having somewhere to state their views independently of the party. *Die Neue Gesellschaft*, however, quickly ran into problems, and only in the second number, amid mounting hostility in the party, readers had to be told that publication must cease until 'normal conditions' returned. It began to appear again in 1905, lasted only a short while, and ceased two years later. It aimed, it said, at 'deepening the cultural life of the nation'. The reference here to things other than politics and economics emphasises, like the corresponding feature of the

Sozialistische Monatshefte, a more than merely materialist and determinist conception of socialism.

As regards Heinrich Braun, it was while he was a student in Vienna that in 1874 he met Siegfried Lipiner, a young man who came to the attention of the Pernestorfer circle as a result of his part in a discussion after a lecture on Nietzsche in the Vienna Leseverein. Lipiner quickly became a prominent member of the circle, whose guiding star, Wagner apart, was Nietzsche, and, with his exceptional knowledge and understanding of Nietzsche, he was soon listened to with particular attention. Heinrich Braun shared his mystical and philosophical interests, and together they read *The Birth of Tragedy*. It was at Braun's instigation, it was said,[8] that Lipiner sent Nietzsche a copy of *Der Entfesselte Prometheus*, which Nietzsche thought well of, and Braun was a signatory of the birthday letter sent to Nietzsche in 1877 by members of the Pernestorfer circle, saying how much he meant to them and how highly they esteemed his work.[9] A fellow member, at the time a medical student who read Nietzsche in his spare time, was Victor Adler, who became Braun's brother-in-law.

From fairly early on Braun had been a keen socialist, critical of the party in some respects, but trusted enough to be made secretary of the St Gallen party congress in 1887. After starting the *Archiv für Soziale Gesetzgebung und Statistik*, he founded another journal, the *Sozialpolitisches Zentralblatt*, in 1892, aiming at social reform by basic changes in the legal system. The purpose, he told Victor Adler, was to 'win over bourgeois intellectuals to our movement'.[10] This reflects the fact that he had a less one-sided view of the role of the economic factor than Marxist theory allowed for, and the importance he attached to the intellectual side of man. He criticised the party for its lack of 'spiritual penetration and depth', and was concerned about the long-term cultural consequences of its need to aim at solidarity and power. He was disquieted by what he called the 'dark urge' generated in the proletariat by the circumstances of capitalism. He was worried, as he said in 1890, by the way, heightened by the pressures of an archaic social order, it 'threatens, or at least conditions, the future of our culture'.[11]

His comments on these problems and their implications came to acquire a distinctly Nietzschean ring, as when he expressed his anxiety about the effects on the individual of a social and political philosophy too concerned with man in the mass, too little with the individual's part in historical change. The need for the individual to bring his energy and will to bear on the course of events, represented for him, as for Nietzsche, a factor of primary importance. Everything, as he was later to tell his son Otto, 'depends on the will that shapes things'.[12] Otto, whose 'splendidly bold manifestation of *Individualität*'[13] he so much admired, appeared to him rather as Nietzschean 'higher man' — the 'fulfilment of my dream of a man of noble being (*Adelsmensch*), who has to enter the struggle of life in magnificent armour, certain of his strength and sure of victory, whether he triumphs or succumbs'.[14] Braun came to share with Nietzsche an admiration of Napoleon, and this directed his attention away from the masses 'to the man who commands them', from the 'anonymous forces of economic development' to the 'power of the man who gave his name to the age', from the 'conditions of production and the laws governing them' to the 'productive achievements of him who made the laws and created the conditions'.[15]

Developments affecting both Heinrich and Lily Braun followed the publication in 1903 of an article in *Die Zukunft* which adopted what was regarded in the party as too patronising an attitude to the working class. It could hardly have been published in the party press, and it was used as a pretext for the Dresden congress to take up the issue of party members writing in non-party, bourgeois journals. The dispute assumed wider implications, among them the general question of intellectuals in the party, which recently had been much under discussion. It had been debated, for example, not long before, at the Social Democratic conference of Saxony, and the fear was growing that they were becoming too influential.[16] At Dresden they came in for some disparaging comments, especially from Mehring, and this led Braun, as a self-declared intellectual, to attack in the strongest terms the 'terroristic régime which Mehring so arrogantly takes upon himself in the party'.[17]

Mehring was one of those for whom people in the party like the Brauns were at best a nuisance and now, as revisionists, they were heretics. The debate on revisionism, a major feature of the congress, produced something of an anti-climax, however, since for tactical reasons most of the champions of revisionism voted in favour of the resolution condemning it. Reporting to his wife, absent from the congress for domestic reasons, Heinrich Braun explained how the vague and wordy resolution had been accepted by the revisionists in an ironical spirit. Lily Braun, having set her face against compromise, was appalled by the news. If she had been present, she said, she would certainly have voted the other way.

The antipathy to intellectuals which was revealed at the congress, and the inflexibility of the party on the revisionist issue, made Lily Braun more determined than ever to highlight the responsibility of the individual in the face of the pressures of conformism and solidarity. Mutual respect and readiness to help one another was not, she thought, enough. Beyond merely fraternal loyalties there was the question of one's responsibility to mankind, and this means — the phrase, we come to recognise, has Nietzsche's stamp — pushing the individual self to its highest possible development. Materialism left people with feelings of longing and homesickness, making them increasingly interested in spiritual and cultural matters. This was why Nietzsche was constantly in her mind around the time of the Dresden congress, amid the difficulties facing *Die Neue Gesellschaft*. His thinking underlined for her now more than ever the significance of the individual as a counter to the pressure of the mass. Society, she felt, was best served when the idea of selfhood was most appreciated and encouraged.[18]

The idea had long-standing associations for her since as a girl she had, as she said, in Nietzsche's *The Gay Science* first heard the call to personal liberation, and this was what she was seeking when as a young woman she had defied an upper middle-class background to become a socialist. Now, as a socialist of many years standing, liberation was again her aim; liberation from too binding and too dogmatic an ideology, from the demands of solidarity, from the grip of a party intolerant of deviance and nonconformism, too much directed at the masses, too headless of the individual.

How important Nietzsche now was to her is emphasised in her *Memoiren* — autobiography cast in the form of a novel, a *Bildungsroman*, and so only partly to be trusted. But it is more likely to be fact than fiction when we read that in her moments of near-despair Nietzsche was her consolation and that on one occasion, taking down their copy of Nietzsche from the shelves, her husband read to her what Nietzsche had said about what he wished for people who matter, that they should suffer and be maltreated. He would not feel pity for them 'because I desire for them the one thing which today can prove whether a person has value or not — namely, that he should stand firm'.[19] When, we are told, an influential trade unionist, committed though he was to socialism as the force which 'welds us all together and in the struggle against our enemies makes us invincible', confessed to her that 'nowadays everyone wants to be something in his own right', the remark delighted her. It reflected, she said, the 'yearning for *Persönlichkeit*', the 'reaction against spiritual levelling which is both the strength and weakness of socialism'.[20] Nietzsche was clearly in her mind too in some comments she made when she was among those who accepted, and was criticised in the party for so doing, an inter-party invitation to visit England. The effect of the visit was to concentrate her mind on specifically Nietzschean ideas. 'The will to power', she said, 'the highest possible development of *Persönlichkeit*, and the Superman as the goal of mankind — what came to my ears in England on this occasion suddenly coalesced in this one great chord.'[21]

She had come to think that she had misled people by talking too much about equality in the sense of everyone having the same possibility of self-development. Now she believed that people evolve in their own individual ways, some more, some less than others. This, she reflected, may make brotherhood between people less frequent, but it makes it all the deeper. It was important to 'respect natural barriers instead of tearing them down', to 'recognise the distance that separates people instead of trying to bridge it with words and phrases'. This passage moves to a Nietzschean climax in the remark that under the mask of brotherly relations we all too easily discount the awe that should be felt in relation to those great in mind and character. One party member commented that he seemed to be hearing Nietzsche's voice. How was it possible, he asked, for her to reconcile her socialism with Nietzsche's doctrines, and, as a tail-piece to one conversation, she heard someone express surprise at a Social Democrat like herself proclaiming, as he thought, a master—slave morality. Of course, she said, she wanted to have nothing to do with the Nietzsche who neither knew nor wanted to know anything about socialism. But, she added, there was more to Nietzsche than that, and 'all his great ideas are part of us ...'.[22]

The quotation continues with a reference to 'the urge towards *Persönlichkeit*, the revaluation of values, the affirmation of life, the will to power'. This reminds one of the mention in that other quotation − when she visited England, the seat of empire − of *Persönlichkeit* in conjunction with Superman and 'will to power'. Remarks of this kind have helped to confirm the belief in some quarters that revisionism nurtured attitudes which weakened resistance to, even encouraged, nationalism and imperialism in Wilhelmine Germany. Stressed in this connection are the shift of emphasis away from the working class, a superior, if not disdainful, view of the masses, loss of belief in historical materialism, idealisation of the role of the individual in history, and, at the opposite extreme from the notion of history as determined by material forces, emphasis on the will. From that point of view the idea, for example, in *Die Neue Gesellschaft* that the revolutionary movement in Russia was the outcome of 'tendencies of the will' stands out.[23] So does its praise of Treitschke as an historian whom 'no reasonable Social Democrat can fail to admire,[24] and its support of Nietzsche's doctrine of the strong and the weak from the angle of its political application in international affairs.[25]

The *Sozialistische Monatshefte* had its dubious features too. In 1899 in the Reichstag, Bebel, concerned for the image of socialism as the party of international peace and understanding, felt it necessary to deny any connection between it and the SPD.[26] What prompted him to do so was an article by Erich Rother, declaring that the German working class had 'vital interests overseas' which would have to be maintained 'in armed encounters with nations open to naval attack'.[27] By this time moreover Josef Bloch, editor of the *Sozialistische Monatshefte*, had himself developed on very different lines from those suggested by the image of the 'good European' which he projected through Felix Stössinger's *Revolution der Weltpolitik*, published in Prague in 1938. Having started out as a revisionist, he had become 'an anglophobe, a protectionist, an illiberal nationalist and a social imperialist'.[28]

The *Sozialistische Monatshefte* thus veered in a direction different from that in which it had started out, and the use to Nietzsche was put changed. Earlier it had used him as an ally of its socialist philosophy. Now, as in some of the articles of Karl Leuthner, a frequent contributor to the *Sozialistische Monatshefte* from around 1907, he was sometimes drawn into the imperialist arguments that occasionally figured in its pages.

Leuthner had written also in *Die Neue Gesellschaft* where he propagated his belief in a policy of expansionism. 'To pursue politics', he wrote, 'means, to quote the young Nietzsche, to tackle the side of things known to be capable of being changed ruthlessly and boldly.' But in Germany, he said, there was always too much talk and too little will.[29] When the *Sozialistische Monatshefte* put forward the notion of a 'continental Europe' (excluding England), Leuthner wrote in support of the idea.[30] Such a policy, he argued, required Nietzsche's 'long will', and, if Germany was to get its just deserts, people had to clear their minds of the thought, propagated by the English, that Germany was an inferior nation. They had to set aside the theory of master-races and lower races (*Pöbelvölker*). But Leuthner was not rejecting in principle the idea of 'masters' and 'slaves' as applied to nations. The implication was that Germany should take more seriously in hand the task of establishing itself in the former category.[31] Germany was to aspire to be the master, and to facilitate this Leuthner wanted the SPD to stop criticising the government's foreign policy[32] though he could, if he chose, also speak in favour of peace and understanding.[33]

In view of the trend of Bloch's own development, one can appreciate his being drawn to Leuthner and Leuthner to him. The same applies to Max Maurenbrecher, whom Bloch had in mind to take charge of a feature column in the *Sozialistische Monatshefte* about art and culture. He was a person, he told Leuthner, 'who is of one mind with me'.[34] Leuthner's own relationship to Nietzsche was hardly more than marginal and incidental. Maurenbrecher's was central, complex and protracted, and for this reason, and because of his other political connections, he now deserves a chapter to himself.

Notes to Chapter III

¹ Cf. Roger Fletcher, 'A Revisionist dialogue on Wilhelmine Westpolitik: Josef Bloch and Kurt Eisner 1907–1914', in *IWK, Internationale Wissenschaftliche Korrespondenz zur Geschichte der deutschen Arbeiterbewegung*, 16 Jg. (December 1890), H. 4, pp. 462–3.

² 1897, pp. 405 ff.

³ 1900, pp. 630 ff.

⁴ 'Darwinistische Asthetik', in *Die Kritik* (2 May 1896), pp. 822 ff.

⁵ 'Naturwissenschaft als Soziologie', in *Sozialistische Monatshefte* (1899), pp. 390 ff.

⁶ *Ibid.* (1900), pp. 76 ff.

⁷ *Ibid.* (1909), pp. 888 ff.

⁸ Cf. Julie Braun-Vogelstein, *Ein Menschenleben: Heinrich Braun und sein Schicksal* (Tübingen, 1932), p. 30.

⁹ Cf. McGrath, *op. cit.*, pp. 70–1.

¹⁰ Quoted in Dieter Fricke, 'Die Gründung der revisionistischen Zeitschrift *Die neue Gesellschaft* 1900–1909', in *Beiträge zur Geschichte der Arbeiterbewegung*, 16 Jg. (1974), pp. 1052 ff.

¹¹ Quoted in Julie Braun-Vogelstein, *op. cit.*, p. 199.

¹² Quoted in *ibid.*, p. 370.

¹³ Quoted in *ibid.*, pp. 374–5.

¹⁴ Quoted in *ibid.*, p. 394.

¹⁵ *Ibid.*, p. 357.

¹⁶ Cf. Richard Calwer, 'Die Akademiker in der Sozialdemokratie', in *Sozialistische Monatshefte* (1901), pp. 319 ff.

¹⁷ *Protokoll über die Verhandlungen des Parteitages der Sozialdemokratischen Partei Deutschlands: Abgehalten zu Dresden vom 13. bis zum 20. September 1903* (Berlin, 1903), pp. 162 ff.

¹⁸ Quoted in Julie Vogelstein, 'Lily Braun: ein Lebensbild', in Lily Braun, *Gesammelte Werke* I (Berlin-Grunewald, n.d.), p. lxxi.

¹⁹ *Gesammelte Werke*, III, p. 505. For the reference to Nietzsche, cf. *Werke*, III, p. 599.

²⁰ *Ibid.*, III, p. 451.

²¹ *Ibid.*, III, p. 521.

²² *Ibid.*, III, pp. 534–5.

²³ Quoted from *Die neue Gesellschaft* (13 June 1906), p. 282, in Dieter Fricke, 'Zur Rolle der revisionistischen Zeitschrift *Die neue Gesellschaft* in der deutschen Arbeiterbewegung 1905–1907', in *Beiträge zur Geschichte der deutschen Arbeiterbewegung*, 17 Jg. (1975), p. 699.

²⁴ *Die neue Gesellschaft* (19 September 1906), p. 452.

²⁵ Cf. Franz Laufkötter, 'Die Taktik des Starken und die Taktik des Schwachen', in *ibid.* (4 July 1906).

²⁶ Cf. Dieter Fricke, *Die deutsche Arbeiterbewegung 1869 bis 1914* (Berlin, 1976), p. 463.

²⁷ Quoted in *ibid.*, p. 463.

²⁸ Roger Fletcher, 'An English advocate in Germany: Eduard Bernstein's analysis of

of Anglo-German relations 1900–1914', in *Canadian Journal of History*, XIII, No.2 (August 1978).

²⁹ 'Eine Politik der vierten Dimension', in *Die neue Gesellschaft*, Bd. 3 (1906–7), pp. 99–101.

³⁰ Cf. Dieter Fricke, 'Die *Sozialistischen Monatshefte* und die imperialistische Konzeption eines Kontinentaleuropa (1903–1918)', in *Zeitschrift für Geschichtswissenschaft*, XXIII (1975), I, pp. 528 ff.

³¹ Cf. 'Herrenvolk und Pöbelvolk', in *Sozialistische Monatshefte* (1909), pp. 475 ff.

³² Cf. 'Umlernen', in *ibid*. (6 May 1909).

³³ Cf. 'Die Aufgabe der deutschen Sozialdemokratie', in *ibid*., 12 Jg. (1908), pp. 1126 ff., where the essential theme is the need to keep the peace, and 'Wozu – Wohin?', in *ibid*., 16 Jg. (1912), pp. 594 ff: 'But the final conclusion remains that Germany must will peace because in the present world-situation peace constitutes Germany's special interest' (p. 598).

³⁴ Letter of 14 May 1909, in the Bundesarchiv, Koblenz, under reference: *Sozialistische Monatshefte*, R 117, fol. 1.

IV

Social Democracy, Max Maurenbrecher, and Nietzsche

Born in 1874, the son of the historian Wilhelm Maurenbrecher, Max Maurenbrecher came to prominence in Friedrich Naumann's Nationalsozialer Verein, was editor of its journal *Die Hilfe*, and in 1900 succeeded to the post of general secretary of the party, to which he had belonged since its inception in 1896.

The Nationalsoziale Verein came into being to cater for the needs of some of the less conservative members of the Christlichsoziale Partei. Its electoral success, however, was minimal. In 1898 it did not gain a single seat in the Reichstag, and in 1903 only one. In the same year it disbanded itself. Most members transferred to the liberal Freisinnige Vereinigung, and a few, including Maurenbrecher, to the SPD. In due course, however, he left the SPD for the conservative-nationalist cause.

Maurenbrecher's shifting political allegiance reflected an element of instability in his character. Naumann was well aware of this and of the somewhat confused element in his idealism. Theodor Heuss, a close associate of Naumann, for a while on the editorial staff of *Die Hilfe* and later first President of the German Federal Republic, knew Maurenbrecher well, and he too stressed this side of his nature.[1] It shows through also in other respects. Pastor as well as politician, Maurenbrecher left the evangelical church in 1907, from 1909 to 1916 served the 'free religious' congregations in Nuremburg and Mannheim, and rejoined the church in 1917, soon after becoming minister of the reformed evangelical community in Dresden.

In an article published in *Die Hilfe*[2] on the tenth anniversary of the Nationalsoziale Verein, Maurenbrecher pondered on the reasons for its failure. Voluntaristic features figure prominently in his argument and they suggest that he had Nietzsche very much in mind.

Political parties, he said, do not emanate from the intellect, but from the will. The motivation to form a political party is always 'simple and strong feeling', not 'logical reflection'. This led him to the view that the Nationalsoziale Verein had been founded at the wrong time, when there was no such 'generally understood and decisive impulse', no need and no public for an organisation of that kind. They were 'Marxists in their way', but the Marxists in the SPD laughed at them, while the SPD went from triumph to triumph. How then could the masses of its followers imagine for one moment that they were on the wrong road, that an alternative party was required? Obsessed with the practical side of the task, 'we wasted years in fruitless political agitation' instead of 'allowing the "new", which was to develop within us, slowly to take shape'.

Very important in this connection is Maurenbrecher's pamphlet *Die Gebildeten und die Sozialdemokratie* ('The middle class and social democracy'),[3] a revised and extended version of a lecture given at a Social Democratic gathering in Leipzig in 1904, just after he had left the Nationalsoziale Verein. In our discussion of revisionism, we noted both a reduced stress on the role of the working class and an inclination to increase the interest of the middle class in the socialist movement. The *Sozialistische Monatshefte* and *Die Neue Gesellschaft* alike highlighted cultural concerns side by side with political matters, and it would be fair to speak of a certain vacillation of emphasis between proletariat and bourgeoisie. Something similar is apparent too in *Die Gebildeten und die Sozialdemokratie*.

This begins by noting, as a self-evident fact, that in all developed countries workers are socialists. Even Gustav Schmoller, Maurenbrecher says, who had hoped to divert the working class from socialism, had had to resign himself to the realisation that this would now be impossible to achieve. Workers are drawn to socialism for obvious reasons; they know that they are at the mercy of the vagaries of the economy, and they are bound to appreciate that as long as there is capital and private wealth they will not get a fair reward for their labour. However, it is not only the working class that is governed by class interests. So too is the middle class, whose special concern is with scholarship and culture. It must learn to recognise how restricted is the scope of these in present society, and once it does so, it will realise that it has interests of its own to fight for, and that socialism is on its side. The inevitable conclusion is that the socialist ideal is not relevant only to the workers; it is the only possible consequence as far as culture in general is concerned.

This helps to show why Maurenbrecher could be tempted to look elsewhere for an outlet for his political energy when the Nationalsoziale Verein sank its identity in a party so strictly aligned to the bourgeois liberal cause. In a sense, therefore, what he wanted was to make the bourgeoisie more socialist; but also, it might seem, his aim was to make socialism more bourgeois. This is suggested by the way the essay proceeds, with Nietzsche playing a crucial role, and in the fourth part becoming the central figure. The question posed there has to do with his relevance for the proletariat.

Maurenbrecher approaches the problem by considering what he calls the subjectivism of the 1890s. People wanted to be 'new at any price'. They scrutinised themselves and their surroundings 'in order to experience new and unknown feelings'. They yearned to 'satisfy the newly awakened longing for an essence all their own, for a vital reaction to everything they experienced ...'.[4] Now, however, he says, people wear themselves out in a hectic concern with outward things, in commerce and the office. They tense themselves up, and their vital life-forces become exhausted. Mankind must therefore move towards a less hurried and deeper kind of existence. This, he says, in quintessentially Nietzschean terms, presupposed a 'new type of man', marked by 'strong feeling' and a 'long will'.[5]

Maurenbrecher, in fact, openly declares his debt to Nietzsche, as the man who 'saw the meaning and goal of life in the "breeding" of this new type of man'.[6] He was, he admits, a great enemy of socialism, a 'pure aristocrat', but his thinking was closely related to the 'ultimate urges and objectives' of the socialist movement, and more so than he or any socialist ever realised.[7] Socialists should therefore not reject him. They should understand that 'he is flesh of our flesh and part of the marrow of our being'.[8] What Nietzsche preaches 'is nothing more or less than the piety of a new age',[9] one no longer dominated by those other-worldly values which have now been destroyed by science and the attention paid to the study of human evolution.

The transition, Maurenbrecher says, has not been without its problems. The first result was resignation and pessimism, but then the consequence of the teaching about man's evolution came to be grasped 'in its positive implications'.[10] This presented a great opportunity, and to describe it Maurenbrecher draws on some of Nietzsche's familiar images and ideas. It was the chance 'to push the evolution of man even further', to see the aim of life in feeling oneself 'as a going over and a going under', as a bridge to new forms,' as consciously collaborating in evolving a new type of man'.[11] He insists that Nietzsche was the first person to make that perspective clear, to establish the 'breeding of the Superman' as the final result of an 'artistic culture'.[12]

However, Nietzsche has too often been misunderstood. His effect has sometimes been to encourage people to turn away from politics to indulge in the pleasures of art. This does not at all suit Maurenbrecher's purpose for if it were to remain a dominant attitude in the middle class, it would be impossible to win it over to socialism. It is unlikely to last, he thinks, and Zarathustra's example encourages him to believe that it will not. He points out that for ten years Zarathustra lived in the enjoyment of his private solitude, but then felt the urge to go among people, to be part of a community; so it is improbable that anyone remembering Zarathustra will forget the claims of active life. At the same time, he stresses that the idea of the

Superman must not be allowed to be confined within a purely subjective context, if the outcome is to be socialism. If you want 'to "breed" a higher type', you must create the conditions favourable to the emergence of 'nobler, freer, superior (*vornehm*) people'.[13] To fashion a new kind of man means creating a new kind of society.

Nietzschean though some of this is, it is also to the eighteenth century that Maurenbrecher looks when he describes what the new society will be like. Echoing the language of that time, he says that it will be one that 'releases all man's powers' and 'allows his innate capacities to unfold'.[14] This amounts more or less to the classical view of the self associated with the ideal of *Bildung* and *Humanität* in the age of Goethe and Schiller. But the stress on self-cultivation was much more subjective than is compatible with Maurenbrecher's desire to safeguard man's activity in society, and so he proceeds to try to give it a socialist flavour. All that this amounts to, however, is that the society he envisages will be a democratic one; the world of the spirit will not be the privilege only of the well-to-do, and man's spiritual capacities will be able to reach their full development also among the lower classes.

All the same, he seems to recognise, as well he might, that he is speaking the language of an essentially bourgeois culture. Many people in the socialist movement, he admits, will have the feeling that in what he is saying 'the idea of socialism is postponed', and that 'one is too much accustomed to see socialism and individualism as pure opposites to want to regard the one as the goal and the other as the means'.[15] But he finds no other possibility of expressing the inmost striving of the working-class movement. What people desire is, after all, the enjoyment of life, culture and knowledge. They want to 'develop the capacities they feel within themselves', to become more inward, more mature people'.

Thus, in *Die Gebildeten und die Sozialdemokratie*, it might seem that Maurenbrecher wanted to be both socialist and bourgeois, and between the two poles his position was clearly as unstable as in the religious sphere, where he vacillated between the desire to be in the church and out of it. He had said that socialism was the goal, individualism the means. Judging by his next work, however, he was of a mind to retreat from the lengths to which he had gone in defence of the latter.

Two years after *Die Gebildeten und die Sozialdemokratie* there appeared his *Die Hohenzollern-Legende*,[16] the title indicating its concern with the implications of monarchy. In *Die Gebildeten und die Sozialdemokratie* he had talked in terms strongly suggestive of bourgeois individualism. In *Die Hohenzollern-Legende* he seems to be going back on his tracks. He wants now to show how little individuals affect the course of things. Development he says, is brought about by the 'conditions which necessarily drive us in particular directions'.[17] With its one-sided class interests, the record of the monarchy in relation to peasantry and proletariat has been shocking. At best, only two possibilities of compromise are now conceivable. One would involve the working class renouncing all political desires, the other a 'truce in a struggle in which neither was able to defeat the other'. However, a young, class-conscious movement would confess failure in advance by accepting either alternative. There remains only ruthless opposition. The working class must fight on, trusting in its own strength. The victorious march of labour is the supreme factor in modern, industrial society, and it is this that 'defines the content of the new century'.[18]

References in *Die Hohenzollern-Legende* to 'democracy and the imperial throne' are reminiscent of the title of Friedrich Naumann's book *Demokratie und Kaisertum*, a third edition of which had just appeared. The connection between the two lies in the fact that in *Die Hohenzollern-Legende* Maurenbrecher is justifying his reasons for breaking with Naumann and the National-soziale Verein. One might well suspect this even without the note in the text to that effect, saying that his book constitutes an 'argument about the past'.[19] The somewhat strident and, by comparison with *Die Gebildeten und die Sozialdemokratie*, more single-minded praise of socialism in this work harks back, one must assume, to the time when he had wanted from the National-soziale Verein 'a clear and unmistakeable commitment to socialism'. But then he had found that most people in it were all too ready to dispense with the Marxist element in socialism to make it more possible to work with the Liberals.

An important factor in connection with both works is the contradictory nature of Maurenbrecher's relation to Social Democracy from the moment he entered it. On the one hand, he was anxious to justify the severance of his connection with the Nationalsoziale Verein, when it turned its face towards liberalism, so he stressed in *Die Hohenzollern-Legende* the Marxist basis of socialism. On the other, in *Die Gebildeten und die Sozialdemokratie* he worked for a more liberal view of socialism than the SPD offered, one better able to appreciate the individual. What he had in mind is clear from the last part of *Die Gebildeten und die Sozialdemokratie* where, clearly under the influence of Nietzsche, he sang the praises of individualism and under-lined the desire to fuse individualism and socialism. This had been in his mind for some time, so that he defined the idea of the Nationalsoziale Verein as a 'new and more embracing kind of socialism than could be represented in its narrower, Marxist form'. Then a little later he noted with pleasure signs of the 'interflow (*Ineinanderströmen*) of Marx and Nietzsche in the direction of the homogeneous and conscious breeding of a higher type of man'.

Mixed up with all this was Maurenbrecher's increasing scepticism about the usefulness of political parties. We can see this from his article in *Die Hilfe* in 1913 where, having broken with the SPD, he looks back on his two 'experiments' and draws conclusions from this experience. One particular conclusion is of special importance. It concerns the role of political parties in general. The problem of socialism, he now thinks, is not one that can be solved within the framework of any party. In any case, a political party is not a suitable sort of organisation in which to study the tasks and difficulties of a still undefined future. His thoughts, radical in their implications, amount to a rejection of political parties as such, of whatever variety. He can hardly not have had Nietzsche's views on the subject in mind when he says that parties are simply more a hindrance than a help when it comes to problems needing honest and penetrating thought. For Nietzsche the sphere of politics stood at the opposite extreme to those aspects of man's existence which in his opinion mattered most. The truly creative people of the past seventy years, Maurenbrecher comments, have not been party-politicians; in this connection he mentions Nietzsche alongside Schopenhauer, Wagner, Marx and Bismarck. Of course, there were plenty of people at the time who, independently of Nietzsche, came to despise politics as compared with the richer life of culture. In Maurenbrecher's case, however, it can hardly be doubted that Nietzsche had helped to foster the idea, bearing in mind his preoccupation with Nietzsche at this juncture.

The year before the article in *Die Hilfe* Maurenbrecher published his most substantial, most significantly Nietzschean, and so from our present point of view most interesting work. This was a book entitled *Das Leid* ('Suffering'),[20] dedicated to the 'interflow of Karl Marx and Friedrich Nietzsche'.

Life, it says, picking up Nietzsche's stress on the role of suffering in human existence, is 'not only springtime and harvest festival'. It is also 'helplessness, pain, incurable disease ... weariness and unsatisfied longing', and 'down the centuries sounds the old sad song of suffering'.[21] 'Life is full of woe (*das Leben ist weh*)' runs one phrase – a little oddly, it might seem.[22] *Weh* is unusual in German as an unattached adjective; one would say, for example, *ein wehes Gefühl*, but hardly *mein Gefühl ist weh*. The effect of placing the word at the end of the phrase and thus marking it out evokes at least an echo of the familiar lines 'Die Welt ist tief ... Tief ist ihr Weh', in the song in *Thus spake Zarathustra* beginning 'O Mensch! Gib acht!'.

In the same context Maurenbrecher writes that 'life is hard — and yet it must be lived. More than that, it must be loved',[23] which is a very simple paraphrase of Nietzsche. Then, follows the advice to 'master life', reinforced with a quotation from *Thus spake Zarathustra* describing every day as lost on which one did not dance, and every truth as false where there is no laughter.[24] Maurenbrecher's injunction is that we must refuse to be crushed by life. We need 'joyous strength', 'zest (*Lust*) to live'. We have to heed 'the great "despite it all", which overcomes all feelings of depression'.[25] Statements like these, and such phrases as 'saying yes to life', 'maintaining a strong and joyous will to life',[26] declare Maurenbrecher's indebtedness to Nietzsche.

Socialists of the first generation, Maurenbrecher argues, were motivated and strengthened by the hope of happiness. They could still believe, even under conditions of deprivation and persecution, that circumstances would change and that they would live to experience the joys promised through social revolution or at any rate in the transcendental bliss of a world to come. The second generation, however, believes in neither of these things. No worker can now imagine that he will live to win the reward of his struggles. For the common conviction of all who call themselves socialists — and here Maurenbrecher's associations with revisionism show through in the doctrine of slow change rather than forthcoming revolution — is that the transformation of society is a long process. The worker alive today therefore knows full well that he will not enter the promised land, and 'from this fact stems the religious problem of the modern working class'. This is the 'problem of suffering man, who realises that he will not personally any more live to see the end of his troubles'.[27]

The chapter entitled 'The overcoming' is crucial in this context. Its point of departure is how Nietzsche 'overcame' Schopenhauer, its larger theme the 'overcoming' of pessimism in general. This, Maurenbrecher says, involves recognising the 'social process as the real content of all that happens'.[28] Nietzsche might not have thought much of that, but Maurenbrecher's argument has Nietzschean ramifications through and through. Pessimism, he says, was the mood of a situation without a future to look forward to. Things are changing now in that, with science, technology and the resources of social organisation, existence now has a 'will', and a future to anticipate and to work for. Suffering and disappointment nevertheless remain an integral part of life. This, it need hardly be said, is quintessential Nietzsche, for whom man's life was tragedy, and suffering, as he said, the inevitable concomitant of all development.

So, in Maurenbrecher's view, we have two choices. One is to try to escape suffering by denying 'willing and becoming' — and he is far too much involved in Nietzsche's voluntarism to contemplate that. The other, which is the way Nietzsche would have seen it, is to welcome it as a way of making growth and development possible. 'Thus, to *want* suffering', Maurenbrecher writes, 'to approve the tragic for the sake of its effect, that is the true overcoming of pessimism.'[29] A person who cannot struggle through to the necessary degree of the 'formation of the will' will either founder in 'Indian pessimism' or 'Christian illusion'.[30] The supreme need, as anyone as deeply enmeshed in Nietzschean thought as Maurenbrecher would have to say, is 'to justify suffering in itself'. Necessary above all is a Nietzschean frame of mind, or, as Maurenbrecher terms it, an 'heroic mood'.[31]

This brings us back to Maurenbrecher's distinction between the two generations of socialist man. Man of the second generation is, like his predecessors, but for a different reason, a 'man of suffering'. He suffers not only in the sense that he will not, as the others thought they would, live to see through revolution the end of his suffering, but also because he does 'not *want* to live to see it'.[32] To face hardship and distress is for him, as Maurenbrecher had learnt from Nietzsche, 'nothing other than the precondition for the strength that shapes things (*schaffende Kraft*) and for growing will'.[33] This insight, says Maurenbrecher, is the 'final, greatest, truest triumph of heroic religion'.[34]

Nietzsche's ideal of man arose ultimately from his concept of the loss of values. In the age of nihilism, without values, metaphysical or otherwise, to sustain him, man would be thrown back on his own personal resources. It was a situation in which energy and will would be decisive, and one to be welcomed as encouraging this result. Maurenbrecher did not think in terms of anything so radical as nihilism, but the loss of two particular values presented for him a challenge of corresponding significance — the double effect of loss of belief in the promise of transcendental reward, compensating the oppressed for their sufferings on earth, and of belief in approaching revolution, destined finally to end their afflictions. From this followed, analogous to Nietzsche's step from nihilism to Superman, Maurenbrecher's idealisation of strength and will.

This being so, it was hardly likely that, in an atmosphere in which nationalism and imperialism were growing apace with the approach of war, socialism would represent Maurenbrecher's ultimate solution. It was more than probable that he would come to see elsewhere than in socialism the basis on which 'heroic man' would best be able to fulfil himself. That was how it turned out. Thus, in 1911 he argued that Germany should initiate a war of aggression against England, which he wanted the SPD to support.[35] When he broke with the SPD, it was because of its opposition to the bill designed to increase the military budget. Now set on the path that was to take him to the nationalist extreme, he joined the Vaterlandspartei when it was founded in 1917, and in the Weimar Republic he was to be found among the Deutschnationale. By this time, however, as we shall see, Nietzsche was no longer a noticeable factor in his thinking.[37]

Notes to Chapter IV

[1] Cf. Theodor Heuss, *Friedrich Naumann: der Mann, das Werk, die Zeit* (2nd edition, Stuttgart and Tübingen, 1949), p. 152.

[2] 'Das nationalsoziale Experiment', in *Die Hilfe* (1913).

[3] Leipzig, n. d.

[4] *Ibid.*, p. 17.

[5] *Ibid.*, p. 18.

[6] *Ibid.*, p. 18.

[7] *Ibid.*, p. 18.

[8] *Ibid.*, p. 18.

[9] *Ibid.*, p. 18.

[10] *Ibid.*, p. 17.

[11] *Ibid.*, p. 19.

[12] *Ibid.*, p. 19.

[13] *Ibid.*, p. 20.

[14] *Ibid.*, p. 20.

[15] *Ibid.*, p. 21.

[16] Berlin, n. d.

[17] *Die Hohenzollern-Legende*, p. 776.

[18] *Ibid.*, p. 779.

[19] *Ibid.*, p. 787.

[20] Jena, 1912.

[21] *Das Leid*, p. 5.

[22] *Ibid.*, p. 6.

[23] *Ibid.*, pp. 5–6.

[24] *Ibid.*, p. 6.

[25] *Ibid.*, p. 6.

[26] *Ibid.*, p. 7.

[27] *Ibid.*, p. 182.

[28] *Ibid.*, p. 168.

[29] *Ibid.*, p. 168.

[30] *Ibid.*, p. 171.

[31] *Ibid.*, p. 171.

[32] *Ibid.*, p. 182.

[33] *Ibid.*, p. 182.

[34] *Ibid.*, p. 182.

[35] 'Was heisst Antimilitarismus?', in *Die neue Gesellschaft*, Bd. 5 (1907), p. 199.

[36] Cf. p. 128.

V
Anarchism and Nietzsche

Nietzsche was highly critical of anarchism, and expressed his contempt for it in a variety of ways. He described it as barbarism, and thought 'lust for anarchy' tantamount to 'chaos'.[1] It was, he said, the 'means used by socialism for purposes of agitation', and it had the same ridiculous dream of 'the "good, the true and the beautiful"', and 'of "equal rights for all"'.[2] Anarchists are 'misbegotten people', motivated by resentment at not having what they feel entitled to. Everything that exists arouses in them a desire to revolt. Georg Brandes, Nietzsche's pioneering Scandinavian admirer, was so struck by Nietzsche's hatred of anarchism that he told him that he thought he judged it in far too rough-and-ready a way.[3] It is hardly surprising, therefore, that of the few studies of anarchism published in Wilhelmine Germany around the time of Nietzsche's death, one does not mention him at all.[4] Another relegates him to a footnote and then merely to discount any connection.[5] Even in George Woodcock's later well-known study of anarchism Nietzsche is referred to only once and then incidentally in connection with Max Stirner.

All the same, anarchism, as a philosophy of extreme individualism, had elements in common with Nietzsche as a radical exponent of selfhood. In its voluntaristic aspects too his thought was in line with some manifestations of anarchist principles. Bakunin, for instance, 'derived the possibility and inevitability of revolution not from the contradictions of the capitalist relations of production ... but from a revolutionising voluntarism which went beyond all mere reflection about what was actually capable of being realised'. Marx said of him that he saw revolution as the product of 'the will, not the economic conditions'.[6] There is no room in the world', Bakunin said, 'for pre-determined plans or pre-established and foreseeing laws.'[7] Nietzsche was opposed to artificial restraints on man's instincts. He saw man as damaged by a tame, mediocre society, and the criminal as a person made ill through the lack of due scope and opportunity for the force of instinct. Ideas of this sort would make good sense to anarchists. Moreover, he welcomed the fact that the 'age of tranquillity' seemed to be over, noting with pleasure evidence of 'anarchistic states of mind' — the mood, that is to say, of protest against too static order — and of other signs of disturbance through which 'personal, virile resilience (*Tüchtigkeit*) ... regains its value'.[8]

If Nietzsche took a poor view of anarchists, they, in fact, often thought well of him. They liked his idea of 'the less state, the better' – the theme of the long quotation[9] which introduced the series of *Flugschriften für den individualistischen Anarchismus*. Quotations from his work were featured in the Leipzig paper *Der Anarchist*. One article, for example, holds out the prospect of man, by the force of his energy and example, opening up the way to the fullness of selfhood. The reference to 'higher man' becoming what he is by his own efforts, and the juxtaposition in the title ('Masse oder Persönlichkeit', 'Mass or personality') also betrays clearly the influence of Nietzsche.[10] 'The coming revolution', it says, 'will be a work of the strong *Persönlichkeit* ... who, working creatively on himself and around himself, marches forward to ever greater perfection, tolerates no power over himself ...'. As to the appeal to anarchist thinking of the 'aristocratic' side of Nietzsche, this is reflected in the case of Emilia Goldmann. In so far, she said, as Nietzsche's aristocracy was 'neither of birth nor of wealth', but 'of the spirit', he was an anarchist, and all true anarchists are aristocrats.[11] It was in very similar terms, and in language clearly coloured by Nietzsche and using one of his most famous images, that the anarchist case was stated in *Der Sozialist*. The conclusion was a call to man to demonstrate whether he was 'bold enough and had the necessary ability' to 'cross and destroy the bridge behind him', the bridge leading from the realm of servants and slaves 'to the limitless sphere, as it seems to us, of *Individualität*'.[12] The Berlin *Der Anarchist* singled out for praise Nietzsche's remarks on the state, religion, law and marriage. Parts of *Thus spake Zarathustra*, it said, were 'absolutely marvellous', containing 'much that we could agree with unreservedly'.[13] How readily Nietzsche lent himself to reference and quotation from an anarchist point of view is seen in an article on anarchist principles in the *Freie Bühne*. 'We stand', it stated, '"beyond good and evil"', morality is merely 'how man arranges the way he lives together', and Nietzsche 'was quite right to see how problematical morality is'.[14] He takes us, said one anarchist journal, to the very goals of anarchism, though there may be nothing specifically anarchist about his themes. Some anarchists clearly thought there was and, as we shall see in a different context, an anarchist like Eugen Heinrich Schmitt could make constant and extensive use of his ideas.[15] A number of these crop up in anarchist contexts, with due acknowledgement, for example 'Revaluation of values', and man as his 'own lawgiver'.[16]

Of course, when anarchists made Nietzsche a witness to their cause, it was not necessarily with strict respect for the evidence in its context. They would isolate aspects of his thought to suit their own purposes. They could be as vague about Nietzsche as were their enemies, who gave the name of anarchism to whatever they disliked and then laid it at Nietzsche's door. To classify any kind of eccentricity as anarchism and blame it on Nietzsche was all the easier since he was now so widely talked about by people who knew so little about him.

In one pamphlet, the writer imagines a German, himself presumably, returning home after some years abroad to find the scene dominated by the 'cult of the self, of one's own *Persönlichkeit*'. It is plain anarchism, he thinks, and it is all Nietzsche's fault.[17] Anarchism could easily serve as a flag of convenience for merely selfish attitudes, as in the case of the 'fanatical anarchists' who, according to Lily Braun, frequented Max von Egidy's household and 'tried to justify the freedom with which they indulged their own petty desires with the excuse that they were living out their *Persönlichkeit*'.[18] Even simple bad manners, with no deeper purpose than to *épater le bourgeois* could count as anarchism, with the culprits instancing Nietzsche in self-justification. One writer mentions someone he knew who thought it one of the prerogatives of the Superman to spit in public and to eat with his fingers. When those nearby objected, he 'proudly appealed to his *Individualität* and to the fact that he was a Nietzschean'.[19] There is nothing more revolting, it was said, 'than when some vain young fathead plays the part of Superman in cafés and pubs frequented by women ... or when late at night some youthful degenerate swanks around in the Friedrichsstrasse "beyond good and evil"' and it was shocking that 'the name and the words of so pure and sublime a spirit as Nietzsche had to put up with being misused in this appalling way'.[20] When the Crown Princess of Saxony ran off with a lover of menial standing, this was attributed to her having been reading his work. By the mid-1890s, the literary cafés in Berlin, Munich and Vienna were said to be 'so swarming with "Supermen" that you could not fail to notice it, and it left one speechless with astonishment'.[21] When in 1897 an anarchist was sentenced for his part in a plot to kill a police officer in Berlin, he defended himself by reference to Nietzsche.[22]

Exponents of eccentric forms of individualism under the banner of anarchism might be excused for thinking that they had Nietzsche on their side; anarchists of the terroristic variety — the 'anarchist dogs', as Nietzsche called them[23] — certainly could not. There is a significant remark in this connection in Przybyszewsky's novel *Satans Kinder* (1897) where one character, a terroristic anarchist, is asked about his attitude to Nietzsche. He answers in very negative terms, having nothing good to say about the kind of anarchism which, it seems to him, could be associated with Nietzsche.[24] In any case, anarchism of the violent kind was weakly represented in Germany, despite the two attempts on the Kaiser's life in 1878. Its German exponents were few and lacked initiative, commented a Prussian police report of 1886,[25] and only a few years later Karl Schneidt commented that 'really purposeful anarchists', with a definite plan in mind 'are in Germany still very thin on the ground'.[26]

The way that Nietzsche could fertilise anarchist thinking of the gentler and more individualistic kind is well illustrated in the case of Bruno Wille, whose development in that direction was remarked upon in connection with the *Jungen* affair. Somewhat surprised by the way people were beginning to talk about him, he denied that he was a 'pure anarchist', 'prophet of the *absolute* rejection of power'.[27] But if some thought he was, he really only had himself to blame, especially as he made a point of praising one notable book by an anarchist about anarchism, Mackay's *Die Anarchisten*.[28] Wille's 'Philosophie des reinen Mittels', it was remarked, looked like an attempt to fuse the ideas of Kropotkin and Max Stirner,[29] and it got a very favourable reception in the anarchist press. Its very title had anarchist associations, suggestive as it is of Bakunin's principle that 'only freedom can create freedom,[30] and of the assertion in one anarchist paper that 'though so many of the best fall victim to the hatred of the privileged and the foolishness of the more humble', mankind can only be saved by the 'purest means', that 'only the *pure* examples of these crucified people have an effect and bring about the transformation'.[31] Wille's *Philosophie der Befreiung durch das reine Mittel* was, it was claimed, 'the first book of an expressly "anarchist" tendency to be published by a bourgeois publisher and to address itself more specifically to bourgeois readers', showing 'that our ideals are beginning more and more to penetrate the ranks of our "enemies"'.[32] With its definition of freedom as the 'possibility of behaving as you wish', as *Schrankenlosigkeit*, Wille, in the essay and in the book, pushed tendencies apparent in his earlier contributions towards their extreme, rejected authority, government, power and the state, and held that only in their absence was 'free, reasonable human community' possible. By this he understood essentially an anarchist community, but he would have no truck with anarchism relying on violence, bombs and murder.

A year after the 'Philosophie des reinen Mittels' Wille published another essay, 'Moralische Stickluft' ('The sultry air of morality'),[33] which had suggested itself to him after reading Adolf Gerecke's recent attack on moral systems in his book *Die Aussichtslosigkeit des Moralismus* ('The hopelessness of moralism').[34] Its title could hardly have failed to catch the attention of someone drawn both to Nietzsche and to anarchism, and keen in this instance to cash in on Nietzsche's exposure of morality. It appealed to him Wille said, 'in these sultry days when it is hard to breathe in air heavy with morality', and when morality is everywhere regarded as mankind's road to salvation.

Wille also had in mind an article by Ernst Haeckel, about a law laid before the Prussian parliament early in 1892 concerning elementary education, which provoked Haeckel to attack the inroads of clerical and confessional policies. Wille's point is that insistence on moral values defeats its objectives. It makes people want to do what is not allowed just because it is forbidden. All it succeeds in doing is to generate hypocrisy. It masks what it sets out to suppress. This might appear as a case for organising society better, but the argument is less a criticism of a particular society than of society as such, the *bête noire* of all anarchists. It consists almost entirely of hypocrites, Wille says, and it holds back the potentialities of man and the creative force of his 'stirrings of the will'.

Wille's voluntarism, as we have seen, was a factor in pushing him towards a more or less anarchist position, and it represented one of his major debts to Nietzsche. His idea of crime in 'Moralische Stickluft' as to a great extent attributable to an 'oppressive moralism' tends towards Nietzsche's theory of the criminal as a 'type of strong man rendered unhealthy by unfavourable circumstances', lacking a 'freer and more dangerous ... form of existence in which all that instinct offers man as regards weapons of self-defence exists in its own right'.[35] It is impossible not to associate with Nietzsche Wille's remark in this essay about the 'individualisation of feeling and thought' as a 'means towards raising the human race', and his idea therefore of morals, rules and taboos as a 'cloying element'. The 'normalising effect' of morality is for him a 'factor making for lethargy', and over such morality, he comments, 'Nietzsche brandishes his flail'. Morality seeks to make people obedient to its own standards 'instead of letting their individual nature freely develop'. Wille sees himself therefore as 'the modern Zarathustra', warning people to be on their guard against 'the good and the just', who 'hate the man who stands alone'.

Wille's voluntarism and his philosophy of the individual converged in the manifesto issued in 1891 by the newly founded Verein der Unhabhängigen, after Wille had left the SPD and others of the *Jungen* had been expelled from it. This marked the shift in the *Jungen* affair from socialism to anarchism, the transition being completed when the struggle for control of *Der Sozialist* ended in favour of the anarchists in 1893. Prominent in the manifesto is the idea of the need to 'individualise the worker', to foster, that is to say, his *Individualität*, and thereby to strengthen his force of will.[36]

The notion that the more a person is truly himself, the more he will be resolved to determine what happens to him is one that we find also with Gustav Landauer.[37] From early on he, like Wille, was a highly sensitive individualist, and as such abnormally intolerant of the demands of ordinary life. (It is a little ironical to find Wille of all people criticising him in due course for his 'nervously exaggerated emphasis on himself'.)[38] His father wanted him to be a dentist, but he would never, he said, take a bourgeois job. His great need was to live out his inner self, and this, it seemed to him, was only possible as a writer. What drew him to the literary *bohème* was what attracted him to Nietzsche. 'Have you meanwhile read Nietzsche?', he asked a friend in 1891, 'if you haven't, you should.'[39] He himself had read *Thus spake Zarathustra* the previous year, when he also started work on his novel *Der Todesprediger*. The central figure of the story is a man who had been won over to socialism by studying Marx, but then abandons it under the influence of Nietzsche. Contemplating suicide, he is saved by a woman who visits him and reawakens in him the idea of 'life' by reading to him passages from *Thus spake Zarathustra*. This, and falling in love with the woman, helps to persuade him that a purely intellectual approach to things is false, that what matters is a vitalistic affirmation of 'life'. This is the essence of Landauer's relationship to Nietzsche. We see it too in his story *Arnold Himmelheber*, written 1893—4, where the idea is that only beyond good and evil is it possible fully to enjoy life and love.

Refusing to contemplate an existence not wholly determined by himself, Landauer rejected the notion of a God endowed with metaphysical authority. The idea of a God expressing man's subjective needs is the theme of his early essay 'Die religiose Jugenderziehung' (1891),[40] on which followed articles in *Die Neue Zeit* in 1892 reiterating his belief in Nietzsche as the exponent of the ideal of selfhood. God, he says in this essay, is what man wants to become and what, true to himself, he will become. Schopenhauer's philosophy now seemed to him altogether too passive. Nietzsche's voluntarism was much more to his taste. A person, he insisted, must be himself; what he becomes depends on what he wants to be.

At around this time the *Jungen* affair was in full swing. Landauer was not one of their number, but he sympathised with them, so he was quick to join the Unabhängige, regarding them specifically as anarchists. When the struggle going on in *Der Sozialist* between Marxists and anarchists ended in 1893 with victory for the anarchists, Landauer, now himself a convinced anarchist, became editor, and the subtitle of the paper was changed to make reference to 'anarcho-socialism'. With Nietzsche's voluntarism a factor in winning Landauer over to anarchism, it came to affect his attitude to Marx, in whose thought, he said, 'flows the vitality of life (*das bewegte Leben*)' and in which he stressed the importance of 'strong will (*kräftiges Wollen*)'. It was too easy, he remarked, to see him in too cold and scientific a light, and to think of socialism in a manner that makes it incapable of educating people to be 'passionate warriors' against the existing order, as 'free individuals with characteristics all their own'.[41]

The negative consequence of so extreme an emphasis on selfhood was a sense of isolation, and in his personal life Landauer was feeling lonely too. An unhappy first marriage, the difficulties (later the collapse) of *Der Sozialist*, and his scepticism now about the chances of radical change, contributed to his discomfort. He adjusted his thinking about the individual accordingly. The 'sovereignity (*Selbstherrlichkeit*)' of the individual', he wrote in 1895, is of the essence of anarchism, but it is 'not absolute'. It has to be fused with the doctrine of the 'sovereignty of the species (*Art*)'. The individual is 'synonymous with organism', a 'part of the community (*Gemeinschaft*)', and 'single individuals, by virtue of descent, milieu, and their qualities of mind and soul, are inseparably connected with each other'. He went on to argue the case in organic terms, on the analogy of nature. Its individual manifestations die, as others are brought to life. It is not the separate phenomena that matter. What counts is the process to which they all contribute, and through which all are superseded.[42]

From about 1898, breaking with the anarchist movement, Landauer began to follow the path that took him towards an essentially *völkisch* philosophy, marked by his participation in the German garden-city movement and by his launching of the Sozialistische Bund which aimed to make the *Volk* the basis of the community. He had ceased to believe that socialism would develop out of capitalism. It would 'grow over and against capitalism', would 'build against it' from a different direction.[43] His ideal now, therefore, was the rural settlement. This shift in his thinking is epitomised in two essays of 1901, 'Anarchistische Gedanken über den Anarchismus' ('Anarchistic reflections on anarchism')[44] and 'Durch Absonderung zur Gemeinschaft' ('Through separation to community').[45]

The first challenges the equation of anarchism and terrorism and asserts the need to act according to the dictates of one's inner self, of the individual will, for 'only from inside ourselves can reality be formed'. Those 'who wish to create life' must be 'born again from within', and accept the obligation — the Nietzschean obligation, one might add — to work on themselves, to 'give new shape to their essential being', to discover within themselves a 'new man'. Such people alone can enable the condition of anarchy to be attained 'in a land yet to be discovered'. Selfhood is still the primary consideration, but on the pattern of dying and becoming, losing one's life in order to find it — and finding it in community. 'Not to kill others but one's own self' will characterise the person who 'works with his own chaos in order to find what is best and most primeval in him, thus becoming mystically one with the world ...'. The second of these essays, complementary to the first, rejects as illusory the feeling that, as an individual person, man constitutes a 'separate unity'. Horrified by such 'terrible isolation' Landauer now renounces all certainty about himself as individual, 'in order that I may be able to bear existence'. So as 'not to be abandoned by the world and by God, I surrender my ego'.

The idea, in the first essay, of man 'working with his own chaos', has its source in Nietzsche, as Landauer acknowledged in his remark about 'this highest moment when, to use Nietzsche's words, man creates the original chaos within himself'.[46] The concept in the second of *unio mystica* – 'the self kills itself in order that the world-self (*Weltich*) may live' – is a different matter. That sentence is repeated in Landauer's book *Skepsis und Mystik*,[47] by which time Eckhart and the mystics, in addition to Mauthner and his theory of language, were more directly occupying his mind than Nietzsche.

This fact, however, should not lead us to discount, even in Landauer's *völkisch* phase, the continuing effect of Nietzsche on his thinking. This is apparent in various ways, as when he describes the type of man who will characterise the 'communities' which now seem to him all-important. What matters, he says in 'Anarchistische Gedanken über Anarchismus', is that 'free people, inwardly firm and confidently in control of themselves, should detach themselves from the masses and combine into new units'. The Nietzschean ideal of 'become what you are' is clearly as far forward in his mind as ever, and we may be sure that, despite the mention of Socrates, it is also Nietzsche he is thinking of in his injunction to 'recognise yourself as you truly are behind all the clutter which you have draped around yourself, and act not according to its laws, but according to the essence of man'.[48]

What happened, as Eugene Lunn puts it, was that in Landauer's *völkisch* phase Nietzsche's insistence on individual self-realisation was given a communitarian direction.[49] If, as Landauer says in the *Aufruf zum Sozialismus*, Marxism was 'the plague of the age and the curse of the socialist movement',[50] it was not least because it placed all the emphasis on historical necessity. It affirmed 'science' at the expense of 'genius' and 'intuition', claiming always to 'know the future ... and how it will come about ... and how it will go on'. Marxists were, therefore, in his pejorative phrase, the 'executive agents of the law of development'.[51] For him, with Nietzsche's voluntarism still an ineradicable part of his own philosophy, it was the human will that mattered. Socialism, he declared, 'is not inevitable', it will come as and when we really desire it. In order that it may materialise, we must – and the phrase is a variation of his (and Nietzsche's) words about the 'chaos within'[52] – 'find humanity within ourselves and then create it afresh. Hence the importance now for Landauer of Mauthner, to whose doctrines he was all the more susceptible because of the extent to which he identified himself with Nietzsche's voluntarism.

The feature of Mauthner's thought most significant to Landauer[53] was, as Eugene Lunn so nicely demonstrates, his assertion that words denote merely abstractions, which then act as a deterrent to the will. We need to believe in something in order to make it possible. Landauer had long been familiar with Nietzsche's insistence on the voluntaristic virtues of illusion. Now in *Skepsis und Mystik* he defends them by reference to Mauthner, though he can hardly not have still had Nietzsche also in mind. To destroy illusions, as Mauthner's linguistic theory set out to do, opens the way, Landauer says, to new illusions, and these facilitate 'new, strong action'. There still lurks something too of Nietzsche's preoccupation with the concept of 'life'; hence Landauer's remark about the 'spirit that bears us along' as a 'quintessence of life', hence too the vitalistic impulse behind his denigrating comments on 'organisations of external compulsion' and the 'sterility' of science, and the idealisation, as against Marxist socialism, of the life-generating force of the *völkisch* community. This, we might say, signified for Landauer communitarian socialism as 'reunion with nature'.[54] Nietzsche did not mean anything as simple as this in his remark in *Thus spake Zarathustra* to the effect that 'we must take possession of the earth again', but it appealed to Landauer at his *völkisch* stage. He quotes it in the *Aufruf zum Sozialismus* in conjunction with the idea 'let the earth have no masters; only then will all men be free', and with the notion that 'the social question is an agrarian question'.[55]

This later part of Landauer's development in the Wilhelmine period is unimpressive, his position adding up to little more than a naive kind of cultural pessimism, that all too familiar conservative cliché of the age. This is reflected in the way he moaned and groaned in 1910 about the 'decay and degeneracy of our time', the 'sickness spreading more and more all around us', this 'ghastly modern world',[56] with himself little else to offer than the demand to 'restore the order of nature'.[57]

This too was where Bruno Wille's thoughts were coming to rest, as is apparent from his pseudo-philosophical novel *Offenbarungen des Wacholderbaums* ('Revelations of the juniper tree'), which appeared in 1901.[58] He had become all too naively the 'enthusiastic poet of nature'[59] — an aspect of his development[60] that Arno Holz turned to comic effect in his play *Sozialaristokraten*, at the same time poking fun at his self-centred concern with *Individualität* and his enthusiasm for Nietzsche as the imagined author of a volume of poetry *Lieder eines Übermenschen* ('Poems of a Superman').

Wille's relationship to Nietzsche however had meanwhile become problematical. Faithful as ever to the concept of *Individualität* which in the first place had drawn him to Nietzsche, he continued to stress the importance of self-determination. But the cult of the self, he now insists, as Landauer likewise had come to do, must be more than 'petty ego-centredness (*Ich-Sucht*)'.[61] This he now rejects as being at odds with the idea of universal harmony which was increasingly occupying his thoughts. He therefore finds unacceptable what he refers to specifically as Nietzsche's notion that the 'order of the stars, in which we live, is an exception', that 'the overall character of the world is chaos into all eternity'.[62] Against this, he sets up a view of the world as an organism which preserves and heightens its own harmony'.[63] The supreme principles of form are embodied for him now in the laws of nature.

Harmony, of course, was what anarchists hoped for from the anarchist community. The free play of selfhood would render otiose all laws and barriers conducive to tension and conflict. So we can still recognise a connection with Wille's anarchist past. His model however was no longer Nietzsche, but Goethe, as the 'great exponent of harmony', thanks to whom 'I have learnt to believe in a harmony in which every little bit of the world, every apparent piece of chance and non-sense, fits in to the general texture'.[64] *Allnatur* and *Allseele* — nature and soul, that is to say, in the cosmic dimension — are all around us. To lose, and in so doing discover, oneself is the joyful culmination of every separate existence.

Im Grenzenlosen sich zu finden
Wird gern der Einzelne verschwinden.

'The individual will gladly disappear in order to find himself in the infinite' — Goethe's words serve Wille as a motif to express the ecstacy of that experience. 'Saved is the man', we are told, 'who has forced his way through the narrow limits of the self, who finds community with the whole, and is happy to become part of the great order of things'.[65]

Nietzsche would have well understood how such a volte-face could come about. 'The richer man feels within himself', he wrote, 'the more polyphonic his inner self is, the more powerful is the effect on him of the symmetry of nature.' Nature, he said, is 'the great means of appeasing the modern soul': 'we listen to the pendulum-beat of this, the greatest clock of all, with a longing for rest, with a yearning to be at home and at peace, as if nature's balance is for us a refreshing drink, enabling us to enjoy the pleasures of our selfhood'.[66]

The position to which Wille and Landauer alike came is thus at the opposite pole to that represented by Auban in Mackay's *Die Anarchisten*. 'Every consistent individualist', he says, 'is an anarchist',[67] which is to say that every anarchist is a consistent individualist. Mackay too was familiar with Nietzsche and was frequently in the company of people who talked a lot about him, like his friends at Friedrichshagen. For him, however, the key figure was not Nietzsche, but Stirner. It was Mackay who rescued Stirner's book *Der Einzige und sein Eigentum* from oblivion, and it was to him that Mackay dedicated *Die Anarchisten*.

Essential in Stirner's thinking was the idea of the individual as aloof from all else, from all other individuals, from all community, absolute and self-sufficient.[68] 'We have to aspire', he said, 'not to community, but to one-sideness'.[69] That was precisely the opposite of Landauer's conclusion. The type of anarchist thinking which Landauer represented — a very German one, one is tempted to say — sought, in contrast to Stirner, the resolution of self-hood in romantic images of integration and totality. Landauer's path led him to theories of *Gemeinschaft* and *Volk*, and Wille's development was in this respect much the same.

This has to be seen in the context of how, amid the disorientating speed and consequences of economic and social change in Germany, the idea of the *Volk*, as an all-embracing and stable community, appealed as a comforting image of assured and inherent essence. In this situation much was made of the concept of the *Individualität* of the *Volk*, of the *Volkspersönlichkeit*. This had various implications. One involved emphasis on the rich diversity within the *Volk* of its parts, its 'individualities', as they were sometimes called, cultural, historical and ethnic. Another was associated with stress on the whole, which was the *Volk*. There is a parallel with the way Landauer's leanings towards autonomous selfhood came to be absorbed in a communitarian framework — and a contrast with Stirner, for whom the individual was self-sufficient, and community irrelevant.

As it turned out, such a view as Stirner's stood less chance in Germany than the *völkisch* alternative, and, even after Mackay's rescue operation, he played, as compared with Nietzsche, hardly more than an outsider's role, at least for a while. Things might have been different if by this time Germany had been familiar with a more self-confident and more realistic individualism, and the prospects of this would have been better if German industrialisation had been able to advance otherwise than under the protection of quasi-feudal traditions and institutions. In the event, as Wilhelmine anarchism clearly shows, an extreme individualism, the anarchist's point of departure, growing fearful of being alone, sought safety in integration and swung from the ideal of autonomous selfhood to what was, in a dialectical sense, its negation.

If there is a parallel in Nietzsche, it is with the unity, described in *The Birth of Tragedy* in Nietzsche's early, 'romantic' phase, of the Apolline and the Dionysian, of the *principio individuationis* and the yearning, in Nietzsche's term, for *Selbstentäusserung*, the urge to discard the self. That idea is expounded at the beginning of Nietzsche's one major work which at the end leads towards an idealisation of the *Volk* as the quintessence of the truly German and its way back to its nature and its roots.[70] Landauer, however, apparently refers nowhere to *the Birth of Tragedy*. It is difficult to imagine that he did not know it and was not influenced by it. Even so, the parallel with his thought, with his resolution of a radically individualist – in his case anarchist – impulse in *völkisch* terms, would not be any less suggestive and important, with reference both to himself and to Nietzsche at the respective stages of their careers.

Notes to Chapter V

[1] *Werke*, III, p. 203.

[2] *Ibid.*, III, p. 845.

[3] Elisabeth Förster-Nietzsche and Curt Wachsmuth (eds.), *Friedrich Nietzsches Gesammelte Briefe*, Bd. 3 (Berlin and Leipzig, 1904), p. 278.

[4] Cf. Paul Eltzbacher, *Der Anarchismus* (Berlin, 1900).

[5] Cf. E. von Zenker, *Kritische Geschichte der anarchistischen Theorie* (Jena, 1895).

[6] Walter Fähnders and Martin Rector, *Linksradikalismus und Literatur*, I (Reinbek bei Hamburg, 1974), p. 25.

[7] Quoted in E. Lampert, *Studies in Rebellion* (London, 1957), p. 135.

[8] *Werke*, III, p. 435.

[9] *Ibid.*, I, p. 684.

[10] *Der Anarchist* No. 29 (Leipzig, October 1910).

[11] *Living my Life* (London, 1932), I, p. 194.

[12] *Der Sozialist* (2 January 1897).

[13] *Der Anarchist* (Berlin, March 1906).

[14] E. Horn, 'Die Freiheit des Egoismus', *Freie Bühne* (1893), pp. 1317, 1318.

[15] Cf. Chapter VI, pp. 64ff.

[16] 'Zur Ethik des Anarchismus', in *Der Sozialist* (14 February 1895).

[17] Cf. M. Helle, *Übermenschentum und Zuchtstaat* (Mainz, 1899).

[18] *Memoiren einer Sozialistin, Gesammelte Werke*, II, p. 429.

[19] Leo Berg, *Der Übermensch in der Litteratur* (Paris, Leipzig and Munich, 1897), p. 216.

[20] Martin Havenstein, *Friedrich Nietzsche: ein Jugendverderber?* (Leipzig, 1906), pp. 22–3.

[21] Cf. Samuel Lublinski, *Die Bilanz der Moderne* (Berlin, 3rd edition, 1904), p. 120.

[22] The Koschemann case. His reference to Nietzsche is mentioned, for example, in the course of a review in *Der Sozialist* of Ferdinand Tönnies's *Der Nietzsche-Kultus* (Leipzig, 1897).

²³ *Werke*, II, p. 660.

²⁴ For Przybszewski's personal account of his early relationship to Nietzsche and the way Nietzsche helped to encourage his inclination towards anarchism, cf. his *Erinnerungen an das literarische Berlin* (Munich, 1965), which was begun in 1924 and first published in Warsaw in 1926.

²⁵ Cf. Reinard Hohn, *Die vaterlandslosen Gesellen: der Sozialismus im Lichte der Geheimberichte der preussischen Polizei 1878–1890* (Cologne and Opladen, 1964), p. 301.

²⁶ Karl Schneidt, *Neue Aufschüsse über die Hungerrevolte in Berlin* (Berlin, n.d.), [ca. 1892].

²⁷ Cf. *Freie Bühne* (1892), p. 412.

²⁸ *Ibid.* (1891), pp. 1251 ff.

²⁹ Max Nettlau Archiv, International Institute of Social History, Amsterdam, reference: MS. 1895 I p. 139 A.

³⁰ Quoted in Fähnders and Rector, *op. cit.*, I, p. 332 n.

³¹ *Der Syndikalist*, 3, No. 26 (1933), quoted in *ibid.*, I, pp. 150–1.

³² *Der Sozialist* (21 July 1894).

³³ *Freie Bühne* (1893), pp. 816 ff.

³⁴ Zurich, 1892.

³⁵ Cf. Werke, II, p. 1020.

³⁶ Cf. Rudolf Rocker, *Aus den Memoiren eines deutschen Anarchisten* (Frankfurt am Main, 1974), p. 72.

³⁷ In my account of Landauer I am deeply indebted, as everyone concerned with Landauer must be, to Eugene Lunn's masterly book *Prophet of Community: The Romantic Socialism of Gustav Landauer* (Berkeley, Los Angeles and London, 1973).

³⁸ Cf. *Aus Traum und Kampf* (Berlin, 3rd ed., 1930), pp. 28–9.

³⁹ Letter from Berlin, dated 23 December 1891, in the Landauer Archiv, International Institute of Social History, Amsterdam, reference: V/x.

⁴⁰ *Freie Bühne* (1891), pp. 134 ff.

⁴¹ 'Die Dühringianer und Marxisten', in *Der Sozialist* (22 October 1892).

⁴² 'Zur Entwicklungsgeschichte des Individuums', in *ibid.*, 2 November 1895.

⁴³ H.-J. Heydorn (ed.), *Aufruf zum Sozialismus* (Frankfurt am Main, 1967), p. 182.

⁴⁴ *Die Zukunft*, (1901), pp. 134 ff.

⁴⁵ Heinrich and Julius Hart (eds.), *Das Reich der Erfüllung* (Leipzig, 1901).

⁴⁶ The Nietzsche reference is to *Werke*, II, p. 284. It is worth noting that the quotation continues with the idea of man as a spectator of the 'drama of his instincts and the most pressing elements of his inwardness', taking stock of them all in order to decide which of the 'many persons' within him is to dominate and what is to be his 'essence (*Eigenart*)'.

⁴⁷ Berlin, 1905, p. 17.

⁴⁸ Martin Buber (ed.), *Der Werdende Mensch: Aufsatze über Leben und Schrifttum* (Potsdam, 1921), p. 76.

⁴⁹ *Op. cit.*, p. 265.

⁵⁰ *Ed. cit.*, p. 67.

⁵¹ *Ibid.*, p. 79.

⁵² Cf. note 45.

⁵³ Cf. Lunn, *op. cit.*, pp. 154 ff.

⁵⁴ *Aufruf zum Sozialismus*, p. 178.

[55] *Ibid.*, pp. 169, 175.

[56] 'Tarnowska', in *Der Werdende Mensch*, pp. 54, 55.

[57] 'Polizisten und Mörder', in *ibid.*, p. 76.

[58] Subtitled 'Roman eines Allsehers', (Jena, 5th ed., 1920).

[59] Wilhelm Spohr, *O ihr Tage von Friedrichshagen* (Berlin, 1920), p. 66.

[60] Cf. also, for example, Wille's poems in his *Einsiedelkunst aus der Kiefernhalde* (Berlin, 1897).

[61] *Offenbarungen des Wacholderbaums*, II, p. 391.

[62] *Ibid.*, I, p. 147.

[63] *Ibid.*, I, p. 179.

[64] *Ibid.*, I. pp. 147, 148.

[65] *Ibid.*, II, p. 391.

[66] *Werke*, I, p. 522.

[67] Berlin, 1912 edition, p. 170.

[68] Cf. R. W. K. Paterson, *The Nihilistic Egoist Max Stirner* (London, New York and Toronto, 1971).

[69] Reclam edition (Leipzig, n.d.), p. 264.

[70] Much the same idea is set forth at about the same time in Nietzsche's *Über die Zukunft unserer Bildungsanstalten*. Cf. *Werke*, III, pp. 218–9.

VI

The subversion debate and Nietzsche

As we saw in the previous chapter, Nietzsche was very much *persona grata* as far as some anarchists were concerned — and in this chapter we shall come across yet another illustration of this. At the same time, he came to figure in government discussions of subversion. There was, however, no connection. The politicians behind the move really knew little about Nietzsche — as little as Nietzsche himself did about anarchism. It was basically the continuing growth of socialism that frightened them. If they referred to anarchism, it tended to be as just another name for the same thing.

These comments are prompted by the so-called subversion debate of 1895 in which, and in the repercussions of which, Nietzsche played a very significant role. The circumstances were as follows.

After Caprivi replaced Bismarck as Chancellor in 1890, Wilhelm II, supported by the army, was anxious quickly to increase Germany's armed strength. Caprivi was not averse to this by any means, but thought that, without some concessions, the proposal would not get through the Reichstag. So he persuaded the Kaiser to accept a shorter period of service and also the reduction from seven to five years of the interval at which the Reichstag could debate the army estimates. With the prospect, as he thought, of the socialists being a greater nuisance than ever after the success of the SPD at the polls in 1893, he had the idea of getting over the problem of the Reichstag by curbing its powers. He was worried too by signs of terrorism abroad, including the murder of the French President by an Italian anarchist. Disquieted by the situation at home and abroad, he called in 1894 for a 'battle for religion, morality and order against the parties of subversion', and in the same year the ultra-conservative Botho von Eulenburg, Minister President of Prussia since 1892, let it be known that he proposed to initiate a bill against subversion in the Reichstag. His hope was that when, as he expected, the Reichstag rejected it, the government could intervene by changing the constitution to the Reichstag's disadvantage. This would provide the opportunity for a general onslaught against troublesome doctrines, solve the question of the Reichstag and bring about the resignation of Caprivi, of whom he disapproved and whose policy of reducing protective tarifs clashed with the agrarian interests with which Eulenburg was associated. Caprivi was not in favour of Eulenburg's proposed bill, and he himself was now constantly under attack from various quarters. Towards the end of 1894 he resigned, while doing his best to ensure that Eulenburg would have to do likewise. The resolve to cut through the problem of the Reichstag, of the SPD and of revolution was now stronger than ever. Prominent in this connection was the Saarbrücken coal magnate Karl Ferdinand Freiherr von Stumm-Hallberg. He had bitter memories of the strike of the Saar miners in 1892 and at the outset of Hohenlohe's chancellorship, he urged drastic action against all forces of subversion. His influence helped to encourage renewed support for the bill which Eulenburg had had in mind. Hohenlohe, however, would have nothing to do with this and he resisted too the idea, now frequently expressed, of manipulating the constitution. But pressure in favour of Eulenburg's bill was such that Hohenlohe found it hard to resist. He arranged for it to be laid before the Reichstag late in 1894, but under the more innocent sounding title of 'Draft of a Law Concerning Changes and Additions in the Penal Code, the Code of Military Law and the Law Relating to the Press'.[1]

Some of those, however, who had supported the bill in the first instance began to waver, and in the end it was rejected. Even Conservatives and National Liberals started to have doubts about it when, as one paper put it, it was coming to be seen as a 'sign of victory for the triumphant power of Rome'.[2] This was a reference to the Centre Party which had been keen on it from the start, and had played an influential part in the original commission. One of the attractions of the bill from its point of view was that it promised to make it easier to act against critics of religion and the church: 'while hitherto only blasphemy was punishable, and then only when found offensive, in future anyone ... is threatened with imprisonment who ... attacks belief in God or Christianity ...'.[3]

This was notoriously what Nietzsche had been doing and so he was an obvious target. He was roughly handled in the preparatory commission and his works were there singled out as particularly scandalous. The ultra-conservative press took up the issue. The author of one article said that some of the 'disruptive influences' were merely misguided, mentioning some liberal theology, for example, and literature glorifying the 'most vulgar human instincts'. This he could forgive, he said, but not the lunatic philosophy exemplified in *Beyond Good and Evil* and *Thus spake Zarathustra*, which should serve to remind the authorities that it is easy to hang lesser thieves and let the big ones get away.[4] It was, however, ironical, as one commentator pointed out, that Nietzsche, a man so hostile to socialism and to everything associated with democracy, should help to provide the excuse for a law directed against both these things.[5]

There were those who thought that this was going to be just another anti-socialist law to replace the earlier one after a decent interval. But, the question was being asked, was it going to stop there? Freiherr von Stumm-Hallberg's intervention in the Reichstag debate, mentioning even Friedrich Naumann, suggested wider objectives than that. Concern was expressed in various quarters, for example, by Conrad Telmann in a pamphlet entitled *Wo liegt die Schuld?* (Who is to blame?) (1895). He had special reasons of his own for registering his objections, as the author of a novel (*Unter den Dolomiten*) about a Catholic priest who abandons his orders because he cannot reconcile the demands of life with the religion he professes. After it was serialised in a newspaper, the editor concerned was found guilty in June 1894 by the Reichsgericht in Leipzig of insulting the Catholic Church, it being assumed that the offending words uttered by the priest ('Your religion is a religion of lying and hypocrisy') represented Telmann's own opinion.[6]

Telmann's pamphlet was highly praised by Karl Helfferich, whose later role in the financial world as director of the Deutsche Bank in Berlin gives his review a rather special interest.[7] Telmann's contribution, he said, deserved attention 'because in this work he puts his finger mercilessly on the delicate spot'. Directed at the 'political unnerving of the German bourgeoisie' the Subversion Bill played on its fear of revolution in order to make it more subservient than ever to authority. Its supporters, Helfferich argued, thought they could do anything with the German bourgeoisie because it had sacrificed its just claims to the political leadership of the people. He was therefore pleased to note the force of public opposition to the bill and the reaction of intellectuals. It was a writers' organisation that printed and distributed Telmann's tract, and there was a petition signed by many writers, including Gustav Freytag, who had been moved to do so by Gerhart Hauptmann, himself named in the Reichstag.[8]

In the academic world a weighty protest came from a body of Berlin professors. Treitschke, the most influential of all, refused to sign ostensibly on the grounds that it would provide grist for the mill of the Social Democrats. In any case, he said, he could not take a tragic view of the proposed changes or see why 'honest radical writers' should feel threatened.[9] By far the most important and interesting contributions by writers and intellectuals to the public debate in 1895 however were three pamphlets, by Eugen Heinrich Schmitt, Michael Georg Conrad and Ernst von Wolzogen. Each attacks the Subversion Bill, in different ways and with different motives, but the common factor in all is Nietzsche.

The real argument in Schmitt's *Herodes oder Gegen wen ist die Umsturzvorlage gerichtet?* ('Herodes or at whom is the Subversion Bill directed?')[10]

begins when Schmitt comes to discuss parliament. This, he says, is one 'grandiose lie', 'the world's great swindle', and run by what, in a favourite term of his, he calls 'the clique', the 'life-nerve of the power-state'. The effect is to make all talk of freedom, of the public good, of love of justice, of progress and respect for truth, mere pretence. There is a limit therefore to the value of parliament as a debating chamber, and this 'lies exactly at the point at which the Subversion Bill aims'. Anyone wanting to unmask 'the great lie' behind the power-role of 'the clique' would find all political parties rising up indignantly in defence of parliamentary government, and treating as criminal anyone who laid hands on 'the web of the whole swindle of "popular representation" '.

Where there is a central authority with an apparatus of power to support it, 'clique terrorism' prevails, and then every democratic appeal to the opinion of the majority is deception. Liberty can only flourish where groups and individuals 'freely form themselves into the whole and organise themselves accordingly'. A harmonious society is possible only on the basis of 'free economic groups', regulating production and distribution in their own independent way. Necessary too is a high moral attitude, leading people to realise the inadequacy of being merely isolated individuals, drawn together only by vulgar material interests. Otherwise selfish, sensual interest will reign supreme and people will fail to raise themselves out of the morass of base material considerations. Any organisation arising freely from within individuals and groups will then be impossible. So the 'divine spirit' must awaken in all, there must be a 'religion of the spirit'.

Idealism, then, is the answer to society's problems. Without it the working class can never escape from its materialism and participate in the 'great revolution of minds'. It can do so, however, if roused to feel conscious of a 'divinity' in which the principle of *Individualität* will be all-important as a protection against the mass pressures all round. If the working class realises this, it can cease to consist merely of 'people laden with suffering under the yoke of capital', and dominated by a leadership denying it moral sublimity and itself aiming to become rulers of society. Liberated thus from the shackles of 'the clique', it could live with the rest of society 'in an harmonious, brotherly way'. 'The clique', then, frustrates the 'awakening of the consciousness of God in man'. It is the enemy of 'the holy community'. So too is the Subversion Bill. It would give added power to 'the clique', and it would open the way to permanent exceptional laws designed to prevent the spiritual revolution at which essentially the pamphlet is aimed.

There is no mention of Nietzsche here, surprisingly perhaps. The stand Schmitt takes against whatever renders life 'uniform, lifeless, without

Individualität' could suggest a connection, as could parts of his argument which invite comparison with Nietzsche's 'the less state, the better', and he is at one with Nietzsche in scorning parliament and party politicians. There is also the idea of man's striving upwards to higher values and nobler forms of existence, albeit with metaphysical implications of which Nietzsche would not have approved.

Ideas akin to these were much in the air at the time, and it would not necessarily follow that they came from him. In this instance, however, there is more to it than that. This begins to emerge if we look first at an essay entitled 'Die Individualität in der Geschichte' ('*Individualität* in history'), which Schmitt published in 1899.[11] This argues that the human, as opposed to the animal, experiences reality as a totality shared by all — crucial terms here are 'living community', 'universal whole', 'cosmic totality'. The 'unfolding of man's cosmic consciousness' is at the same time an 'unfolding of himself'. At the centre of his single consciousness, we are told, he fuses the antimonies of 'selfhood (*Selbstheit*)' and 'universality', thus providing the basis on which alone a harmonious community of individuals can take shape. This merely recapitulates themes from the earlier pamphlet, and in the same hazily metaphysical language — one begins to appreciate how one periodical turned down a contribution from Schmitt on the grounds that readers would get about as much from it as if the pages had been left blank.

Two consequences follow for Schmitt from this application of the idea of *Individualität*. One is that it is no longer correct to believe that milieu and *Zeitgeist* are the decisive factors in history, with the individual fading to insignificance. The other is the eminently Nietzschean association of weakness and decay; one form of culture breaks up and 'higher life' knocks 'at the door of history'. The new development inevitably runs up against powerful interests, anxious to preserve things as they are. Gradually, however, the 'heroes of the new cultural idea' gather an èlite around themselves, small at first, but growing as time passes. The point then comes when they tear the ground from under the 'principle in decline' and 'conquer it for the principle replacing it'. Like Nietzsche too, Schmitt is encouraged by the promise vouchsafed in Greek life and culture. Like him also, for whom the 'higher man' is the response to the challenge of a world where God is dead, he looks forward to an age freed from Christian metaphysics, and so better able to move towards the 'self-awareness of *Individualität*'.

Shorter and more concentrated as it is, this article highlights all the better essential features in the argument of *Herodes*. It implies notions of a teleology of history alien to Nietzsche, but it makes the parallels with him the more striking. They can hardly have been accidental. In fact, we know that

Schmitt had been involved in studying Nietzsche and was deeply attached to his philosophy.

This is clear from his review that year, in the same journal, of Hans Gall-witz's recent book *Friedrich Nietzsche: ein Lebensbild*. Here Schmitt fully identifies himself with Nietzsche's thinking and speaks of him enthusiastically as one who set out to create a new and higher culture in which man could at last breathe freely and develop his own divinity'. This and other features of the Gallwitz review are so similar to *Herodes* that, if they are directly related to Nietzsche, the corresponding aspects of the pamphlet must be so too.

We suggested a comparison between Schmitt's use of the concept of *Individualität* in *Herodes* with Nietzsche. Now we can be confident of the connection, for when, reviewing Gallwitz, Schmitt speaks of the 'universal life of *Individualität*', a notion familiar in *Herodes*, it is Nietzsche he is talking about. Nietzsche expounds the idea 'in his teaching about the Superman or man as "God", that is to say, about man with universal self-awareness, who merges cosmic totality with selfhood (*Selbstheit*)'. Moreover, by the time Schmitt came to review Gallwitz, he must have been immersed in Nietzsche for some while, since he himself published a book on Nietzsche in 1899.[12] Nietzsche is there described as a man who leads us over into new and hitherto unsuspected areas, into a new world of feeling and a quite new attitude to life. He is the 'illustrious visionary and prophet' who sees a new world of spirituality, bathed in 'sunlight and the splendours of the virgin forest'.

Nietzsche's world, as imagined here, is, of course, the very opposite of Schmitt's picture of contemporary society in *Herodes*. Characteristic of the latter is Schmitt's abhorrence of 'power', and this, in conjunction with his contempt for parliament, his near-mystical exaltation of the individual and his preoccupation with the 'free community', derives from his anarchist connections. Under the name of Eugen Bulla he had contributed to Johann Most's anarchist journal *Freiheit*, and articles by him appeared in *Der Sozialist* after it had adopted an anarchist position. One of these, sketching the nature and inevitability of anarchism, is about anarchism and religion, and it shows a clear relationship to *Herodes*.[13]

By comparison with other alternatives, anarchism here represents for him the 'burgeoning of a new life of the spirit'. Social Democracy, he says, makes people 'social atoms', theology stresses the 'nullity of the individual, reducing him before God to dust and nothingness'. Anarchism, however, the philos-ophy of the 'majesty of the individual', champions respect for the 'supremacy of *Individualität*'. The community it encourages does not depend on the force of external, mechanical means, but stems from 'within the individual'. Schmitt instances Proudhon, Stirner, Bakunin and Kropotkin — not Nietzsche

— but they were the more obvious examples to cite in an anarchist journal. Nietzsche, however, is not far beneath the surface of the argument, as when, in one passage dominated by an aristocratic individualism, the themes of 'heroism' and 'moral nobility' converge in praise of anarchist man and of the revaluation of values to be expected of him when he reigns supreme.

Briefly then, it was above all Nietzsche's hostility to the 'new idol', the state, together with his affirmation of Nietzsche's 'sovereign individual',[14] that led Schmitt, as an anarchist, to admire him, and it was as an anarchist that in the Subversion Bill he saw the 'power state' brutally imposing itself on the individual. This Schmitt then grandly elevates to the status of an 'ego ... as vast as the world', and as such, ultimately, the agent of the great spiritual revolution on which he pinned his hopes for the future. The Subversion Bill was for him the enemy of that utopia, Nietzsche its friend and ally.

The second figure with whom we are concerned is Michael Georg Conrad. He had different reasons for attacking the Subversion Bill, but it angered him just as much. So he promptly set off on a lecture tour to speak against it in several German cities in January 1895, in Frankfurt, Stuttgart, Mainz, Mannheim and Würzburg. The extended outcome of his address was *Der Übermensch in der Politik* ('The superman in politics').[15]

He had been a devotee of Nietzsche, Conrad tells us, since as a boy he read the opening pages of *The Birth of Tragedy*.[16] Thereafter his attitude remained almost consistently one of admiration. Already in 1886, when Nietzsche was less widely known, he was quoting *Thus spake Zarathustra* in a review.[17] Three years later he recommended *The Genealogy of Morals* as 'one of the boldest and cleverest publications in the sphere of philosophical speculation'.[18] When Hermann Türck's *Friedrich Nietzsche und seine philosophischen Irrwege* appeared in 1891, he scornfully commented on the gulf separating its author from the sublimity of Nietzsche's genius.[19] Despite occasional criticism of Nietzsche, Conrad's relationship to him was still enthusiastic when in 1891 he published *Die Sozialdemokratie und die Moderne*, and he went on speaking of Nietzsche affirmatively in *Die Wage* in 1899 and in *Die Insel* in 1900. There is thus a steady pattern in his attitude to Nietzsche — excepting virtually only *Der Übermensch in der Politik*.

This opens with a biting critique of Bismarckian Germany. The German nation, he said, had allowed itself to have imposed on it a 'tutelage ... unparalleled in history', which had engendered a sense of subservience and receptivity to military discipline and had undermined Germany's trust in its own strength and dignity. The Prussian victory of 1871 had prepared the way for the police powers of Bismarck's dictatorship, for its brutal policies, for the Anti-Socialist Law, for the *Kulturkampf* and for the prosecution of people charged with insulting the monarchy. Bismarck was engaged in trying to subdue his own people, and the cultured part of society supported all the reactionary tendencies. Parliament, weakened by electoral wrangles, consisted only of people representing special interests and cleverly doing what their parties expected them to do. Under this system of drilling and pressurising people, Bismarck was able to cloak his arbitrary rule under the appearance of constitutional rectitude.

It was in that situation, Conrad recalls, that he launched *Die Gesellschaft* some ten years earlier, causing panic, as he liked to think, in Bismarck's 'Reich of the philistines'. There was an almightly clamour, as always 'when what is old and *passé* has become an intolerable burden for what is vital and creative'. People called for 'nature' and 'truth' against 'hollow idealism'. What was demanded was the 'full living out of *Persönlichkeit* ... release of the powerful force of instinct and passion, beyond good and evil, beyond all narrow-minded morality and traditional authority'.

The cultural possibilities here described are thus set forth in terms close to Nietzsche's rejection of idealism, to his insistence on the release of self-hood, to his affirmation of instinct and to his challenge to morality. If these possibilities did not materialise, Conrad now says, it is Nietzsche himself who must be blamed, or at any rate attitudes derived from misunderstood Nietzscheanism and a 'foppish' imitation of Zarathustra. Under Nietzsche's influence people ranged themselves loftily above the real world and looked down disdainfully from the clouds on political democracy. Young poets and artists particularly felt 'indescribably aristocratic', cultivating airs of superiority that often belied their social origins and the kind of existence they actually led. Their form of 'Supermanhood' was the cult of art as absolute, and their image of themselves was as 'we sublime people', for whom ordinary mortals meant 'mass values' and the 'feeling of the herd'.

Thus (and with a tiny, unrepresentative and, one is bound to say, wayward section of the German population in mind) Conrad deduces that Nietzsche's philosophy had encouraged men to turn their back on politics at a time when, it is clearly implied, the Subversion Bill made it all the more necessary for them to engage themselves. What, Conrad asks, will these ethereal souls do now that the 'upper ten thousand' are 'showing us the writing on the wall of the devil of subversion' in order to put the police at the throat of freedom in art and poetry? Will 'our aristocrats of the pen and the paint-brush', in their cloud-cuckoo-land of culture, grasp 'this new signal for battle from the forces of reaction ...'?

The contrast with what Conrad had been saying not so very long before in *Die Sozialdemokratie und die Moderne* could hardly be more striking. In *Der Übermensch in der Politik* he insists, in a politically bad situation, on the need for the writer not to turn his back on politics. In *Die Sozialdemokratie und die Moderne* he had denied the relevance of politics to art, adjuring the artist not to let himself be determined by what the 'party score (*Parteipartitur*)' laid down. In the one he expresses contempt for those who, in the wake of Nietzsche, viewed the artist as autonomous in a spiritual world of his own. In the other, he had idealised the artist as the 'purely free man', and art and literature as self-justifying. In the later work he rejects Nietzsche for his aristocratic and elitist values, while in the earlier work he praised him for this very aspect. 'The process of growth of the modern movement towards blossom and fruit', he had said, follows the Zarathustra call "upwards" '. His concern then was with the person, familiar in Nietzsche's scale of values, who 'longs for the heights'.

This astonishing change in Conrad's view of Nietzsche in *Der Übermensch in der Politik* can only be understood in the light of his political development around this time, which he described in an account of his Reichstag candidature.[20] Coming, he says, from a rural and peasant background, he was not attracted to any party given to high-sounding talk. This was why he had now joined the Deutsche Volkspartei, which in *Der Übermensch in der Politik* is described as embodying 'simple democracy with rejuvenated force'. What attracted him about it, he says, was the interest shown there in practical tasks and economic and social realities, 'without too much emotion and bragging, without somersaults and waffling about being infallible'. Hence he now attacks what he calls 'anarchistic man', as someone preoccupied only with himself, regarding himself as miles above the ordinary people to whose long labours we own culture as it is today. He was 'without organic connection with natural developments and without any firm basis in the general cultural life'.

The Deutsche Volkspartei was supported mainly by the rural and small-town petty bourgeoisie, whose interests it represented against large-scale industry and monopoly capitalism. It existed virtually only in southwest Germany, because of the social structure characteristic of that area, with industry scattered and poorly developed. Small and middle-sized property ownership was typical. Even the craftsmen were mainly at the same time small farmers.[21] Accordingly, in *Der Übermensch in der Politik* Conrad is particularly concerned for people like craftsmen and peasant, threatened by monopoly capitalism. It is these that he is thinking of most of all when he describes democracy as best suited to giving scope to the 'strong individual natures' in society and to allowing all to participate in the 'free unfolding' of society in all its parts. That it is this petty bourgeoisie he has in mind when he speaks of the 'ideals of the bourgeoisie'[22] is clear from the fact that he immediately goes on to speak of the 'economic liberation of those who earn their living from small businesses of their own, especially the peasantry', best achieved he thinks, through the Deutsche Volkspartei. If he also expresses concern for the 'masses' and their 'inescapable demands', it is because, likewise disadvantaged by the disproportionate power exercised by industry and high finance, they are natural allies. All must have the chance to raise themselves up and fulfil themselves — so any division of people into 'masters' and 'slaves' conflicts with Conrad's view of things. The 'herd animal' must be able to become more than that, and this is not possible unless everyone is in a position to be able to develop the 'power latent within him'. Then, Conrad goes on, he will be able, 'with everyone else, under the same conditions and from the same position, to enter the competition and gain the position in society which befits his particular powers and abilities'. Democracy, properly understood, moulds the 'herd animal' into the 'free, self-aware *Persönlichkeit*, makes him conscious of his own dignity' and absorbs him into the company of 'higher men'. The operative principle is what, in another Nietzschean phrase, he calls 'selection upwards'. People other than the powerful and the privileged can thus win their way to 'spiritual excellence (*Vornehmheit*)'.

Thus, Conrad defends the interests of the petty bourgeoisie against the pressures of industrial and financial concentration. But from another point of view he accepts the consequences of economic imperialism. This is seen in his approving review in 1897 of Johannes Wernicke's praise of protectionist policies in his *System der nationalen Schutzpolitik*.[23] He consents to Wernicke's idea that any 'politics of *laissez-faire*' is outdated. Everything nowadays is a 'question of power', 'everything is business', and the important question is 'how do I assure myself of the best advantages'. One 'does not live for oneself as individual', what one is 'one owes to one's nation'. 'As between single people', he says, quoting Wernicke again, 'so it is between peoples and nations as whole units, where the same competitive procedures operate.' 'Did you hear that', he comments, 'you anarchistic, individualistic Nietzscheans?' Nietzsche having proposed 'the less state, the better', Conrad therefore asserts, in the Wernicke review, the opposite, 'as much state as possible' — the state, that is to say, as a means of 'protection', a *Schutzverband*.

It must, however, leave the inner processes of society to develop in their own individual way. The history of a people, Conrad says in *Der Übermensch in der Politik*, is 'natural history', and 'nature does not let itself be forcefully hurried along'. So, speaking of the *Volk* in nature's terms, Conrad compares it to a tree. A healthy tree is one which in all its parts, from the roots to the uppermost branches, 'grows in a uniform way'. It must have more than just a 'beautiful top', a few lush branches and a lot of dead ones, and 'the only *Volk* that can count as a correct, natural *Volk* is one which grows full of sap and strength throughout, equally splendid and beautiful in all its parts'. The tree that is the *Volk*, that is to say, must not be allowed to flourish only at the summit.

It is because he is thus opposed to the power of the few at the top that he is all the more ready now to condemn Nietzsche as the ally of autocracy. He had not seen Nietzsche in this light before. If he does so now, it is because of the Subversion Bill and the encouragement it would give to those attracted by the 'excesses of power in the hands of the masters'. 'A wonderfully gifted, but one-sided and in the end mad philosopher' he says, 'has written out the score for this new leitmotif of our latter-day Renaissance, which outdoes the original, this *überrenaissancelte Renaissance*.' Some of the 'artistic Superman-dreamers' may follow the principle of 'keep off politics'. Others however, impressed by the 'devilish logic of the glorious right of the stronger', see no reason why the 'will to power' should be inhibited by 'democratic backwardness'. So it is to Nietzsche's anti-democratic attitudes that Conrad devotes the most hostile section in *Der Übermensch in der Politik*, painting a picture of a philosopher whose 'eye rolls in aristocratic madness' and who 'lost all respect for the people and all sense of decency'. For if the Subversion Bill became law, he says, the result would be to treat monarchy and Reich as an 'inviolable entity'. This would encourage the ruler to take 'all power into his hands' and thus to establish the principle of the Superman as an 'infallible power omnipotent in the class-state', and embodied 'in the dictator on the throne'.

So, not only had Conrad's image of Nietzsche changed, but also his view of Bismarck and the Kaiser. In *Der Übermensch in der Politik* he castigates Bismarckian Germany. But he had earlier declared his 'unshakeable faith in the extraordinary powers of development of our young Reich', and had spoken with veneration of Bismarck himself as 'this phenomenal German', this 'heroic' man who 'with a strong arm had intervened in the fate of nations', making Germany 'united, strong and great'.[24] In *Die Sozialdemokratie und die Moderne* Conrad's enthusiasm for the Kaiser was undiminished, but in *Der Übermensch in der Politik* he is censured for behaving in ways 'which usually only stem from feelings of great superiority and independence'.

This is very different from what he had written in 1890 when he praised a Danish article lauding the Kaiser for his concern about the working-class movement. This was the aptest thing, he said then, that had ever been written about the Kaiser and the social question. Conrad may well have liked the article all the more because it had said that a peaceful solution of that problem demands 'a sort of aristocratic radicalism'. The phrase, an echo of the title of Georg Brandes' well known essay on Nietzsche,[25] exactly matches the spirit of *Die Sozialdemokratie und die Moderne*.

Moreover, by the time Conrad was faced with the problem of the Subversion Bill, events had taken place nearer home which must have combined with the impact of the bill to heighten his disquiet about what was happening in far-off Berlin. On his own doorstep, so to speak, there had been, in flesh and blood, the living example of those 'absolutist cravings' he spoke of in *Der Übermensch in der Literatur*, that 'autocratic arbitrariness of attitude which the experience of the Subversion Bill led him to attribute to Bismarck and the Kaiser. For it was only four years after Conrad settled in Munich in 1882 that Ludwig II of Bavaria was deposed, after squandering the state's financial resources on extravagant architectural and artistic adventures and haughtily defying his ministers and the constitution. He is the central figure in what must be regarded as the literary postlude to *Der Übermensch in der Politik*, Conrad's novel *Majestät* (1901).[26]

Here, in contrast to his father, portrayed as a modest and constitutional monarch, the friend and helper of his people, Ludwig II is painted as distant, solitary and romantic. In his father there was not 'a trace of creative fantasy', but his son's imagination ran wild. For him art was all, the 'great liberator', the 'eternal redeemer'. His development, unfolded often in interior monologue which constantly echoes Nietzsche, is towards a megalomania so extreme as to make it seem that he had been mad all the time. Already at his accession he sees himself as a 'sovereign ... in the glorious autocratic sense of the age of powerful rulers', and he views himself as 'poised on the highest rung of glory, on the pinnacle of the state, responsible only to himself and his God'. A sort of caricature of a Superman, he is drawn to Wagner as 'the Superman to match his royal dream-image of himself'. People might complain about his ever more exorbitant building plans, but, seeing himself as a 'greatly exceptional man', he is 'a law unto himself', caring nothing about 'the all-too-many'. In his philosophy the quality of nobility elevates, to be on high is to be lonely, and to be solitary goes against the instincts of the masses. Therefore, in his system of values, 'it is time's wish that everything noble should be dragged down, but the man of noble nature wants the best to have the opportunity to rise up from the mass and live their own creative life in beauty'.[27]

Ludwig II thus rules 'with the mystical glory of a man on his own'. The phrase comes from *Der Übermensch in der Politik*, but it fits the Ludwig of *Majestät* perfectly, and it pinpoints the complementary nature of the two works. For, as is stated in the novel, a ruler in a modern state has to be modest and restrained as far as personal or dynastic or personal pride is concerned, and he must keep strictly within the limits of the constitution. There is no room for a 'turbulent, self-righteous person ... at the head of a state that needs soberly to concentrate on work'.

By comparison with Schmitt and Conrad, Ernst von Wolzogen's contribution to the public debate about the Subversion Bill has an altogether lighter touch and, though it describes itself as 'a serious admonition to the ruling classes and to the German nobility in particular', a refreshing sense of humour. Its aim is to elucidate 'the causes of the miserable helplessness which the ruling classes have shown in relation to the spirit of the time by supporting so silly a government proposal' as the Subversion Bill.

Linksum kehrt schwenkt – Trab! ('Left about-turn, wheel - trot!') – an improbable title, it might seem, for a political tract – begins by remarking that those who legislate are obviously of the view that all 'would gladly pay their taxes and recognise their princes as chosen by God to be the hereditary tenants of all wisdom and all human love', if it were not for the troublesome few anxious to persuade them that no thinking person should be thus contented. Our 'good wise and gracious government', doing its best 'to enable its faithful subjects to lead a contented existence', clearly cannot believe that anyone could ask for more. It is only, it thinks, because some people unscrupulously preach seditious doctrines that more and more Social Democrats get elected to the Reichstag each year and that the people become less and less satisfied. To those in high places it seems that the only way to stop the rot is to muzzle anyone with new ideas. So, Wolzogen thinks, it must be against writers and the press that the Subversion Bill is aimed in the first place. Those who express themselves by word of mouth, political speakers and the like, are, after all regarded as second-class people, and it is from the printed word that they are supposed to get their foul beliefs. When a few writers and agitators come before the courts, the judges look upon them as different from ordinary people, as over-excited ragamuffins, with nothing to lose, and so able to mock 'the most sacred possessions of mankind'. They fail to grasp that such people only express in cruder form what the majority of intelligent people think and take for granted in the modern world. The way they look at these people is all the more ridiculous because in between the simplest peasant, from whom the ruling classes tend to get their image of the common people, and their own 'classically trained magnificence', are to be found all those people conditioned by ordinary life, and it is they who really determine the character of our time.

Nietzsche is clearly in Wolzogen's mind as one of the 'lonely thinkers' for whose 'new thoughts' all those people 'struggling in their bewildered way' are in most cases already prepared, and it is from Nietzsche that he takes the idea central to his criticism of the nobility. As a protagonist of a Nietzschean ideal of aristocratic *Vornehmheit*, Wolzogen censures as false and absurd the kind of aristocracy that the nobility cultivates. It is merely pride in an old-fashioned 'mental uniform'. The more archaic it is, the more refined it is held to be. In that world no one wanting to be included among the select few dare deviate from the ways of his peers. To have an opinion of one's own counts as impertinent and vulgar. The 'upper ten thousand' feel infinitely superior to the mass of the people and reach the silly conclusion that it is only by clinging to old authority that it is possible to keep your boots clean and your manners as they should be. Hypocrisy becomes a virtue and lack of ideas a good thing.

Wolzogen was himself an aristocrat by birth, and from his point of view the nobility does indeed constitute a special type of people. It had grown up in conditions of freedom and over a long period had occupied leading positions in war and peace. It had thus been privileged to be able 'to develop its capacities in a many-sided way' and to produce mentally and physically tough, strong people. Wolzogen may have idealised the role of the nobility in history,[28] but when he said that it brought the punishment of revolution on itself, and took the opportunity to warn it of the legitimate and widely-shared pressure from below for more enlightened policies, he was clearly right. Otherwise, he was sure, the result could only be the triumph of Social Democracy and a falling back into mindless barbarism.

Wolzogen's argument is couched in language heavily stamped with the imprint of Nietzsche. If what he fears happens, he says, we should be subject to the 'rule of the ridiculously unscientific axiom about the equality of all' and fall victim to the brutal idea of the state as the only employer, teacher and paymaster of us all. *Persönlichkeit* would then vanish under the pressures of 'an intolerable tyranny of numbers'. This would be a society from which 'no genius could possibly arise' and where the opposite of *Vornehmheit* would prevail.

Hence Wolzogen's call to the nobility to shed the armour of prejudice, to listen to what 'new tidings' the present day has to tell, and to become 'modern people'. The same applies to the monarchy. What is needed is a 'modern mind on Germany's imperial throne', appealing to the sense of 'genuine *Vornehmheit*' and so able more effectively than any general to protect his throne and country against the menace of a 'fanaticised mob'. Such a monarch, committed to the notion of spiritual freedom for all, would create a new aristocracy and with its help lead his people to fairer victories than those to be gained by force of arms. This new 'aristocracy of the spirit' would bring about the 'revaluation' of old and moribund values, and that would be a 'loyal and sensible kind of subversion'. As the pamphlet nears its end, with the ground prepared by references to *Vornehmheit*, 'aristocracy of the spirit' and 'revaluation', Nietzsche is named as the model. 'If we extract from Nietzsche', Wolzogen writes, 'his lyrical raving about the Superman ... what remains of his teaching is exactly what I have recommended here ....'

Wolzogen's new aristocracy however was not to be as circumscribed as his declared belief in the nobility of blood might suggest. As a nobleman, he identified himself with the hereditary nobility because, ideally at least, it pre-eminently embodied the quality of true *Vornehmheit*. As a writer, however, his links were with the bourgeoisie, to which belonged, writers and intellectuals apart, those practical men of affairs whom he plays off against the pretentious, unworldly refinement of the aristocracy. This had once been in a special position to be able to produce rounded, capable people. But now he points out, the descendants of the old burgher families have come to share similar advantages and so qualify as belonging to the aristocracy of birth. The old difference between noble and bourgeois therefore no longer exists. So Wolzogen's perspective is of a ruling class fusing aristocracy and bourgeoisie, each with its own contribution to make, each partaking of the virtues of the other, and together providing the basis of a modern and viable *Vornehmheit*. This was his ideal as an enlightened aristocrat, to whom Nietzsche was guide, philosopher and friend.

The light-hearted, almost jocular title of Wolzogen's pamphlet hints at the irony of the fact that those to whom it is addressed, for all their highfalutin pretensions, live confined within a world of horses and cavalry commands. The title, and at times the style, have something in common with the tone of Das Überbrettl, the short-lived cabaret-type theatre for the creation of which Wolzogen is now best remembered. The term *Überbrettl* plays on *Übermensch*, implying both relationship to and advance beyond — the overcoming of, one might say, in Nietzsche's language — the cruder and more 'popular' stage show or *Brettl*. From *Mensch* to *Übermensch*, from *Brettl* to *Überbrettl*, that is the progression, and the parallel with Nietzsche betrays his influence in the background. Wolzogen, in fact, had immersed himself in Nietzsche in making his plans for Das Überbrettl,[29] and Nietzsche was the inspiration of its characteristic elegance and refinement.

For it was Nietzsche who 'once again found a place in art for grace (*Anmut*)',[30] and it was in connection with Das Überbrettl that he talked about how he had succumbed to Nietzsche's idea of 'Dionysian man, of the dancer, of the *gaya scienzia*, of the taming of the blond beast through a culture of grace and aristocratic refinement'.[31] The last part of the quotation parallels the principle at which *Linksum kehrt schwenkt – Trab!* is directed. The aristocracy needs, if not to be tamed, to be civilised. Its *Vornehmheit* is that of people whose haughty values lack any basis in real life – the *Über-*, so to speak, without the *-brettl*. Stiff and unbending, it lacks the natural and easy grace of the dancer and the dance.

When it comes to a concluding assessment of the three writers dealt with in this chapter, and bearing in mind the nature of Nietzsche's impact in relation to authority and power, Schmitt is a fairly straightforward case once one has penetrated the haze of his often dotty idealism. Wolzogen is not a difficult case either, with his criticism of establishment values motivated by a desire, ultimately conservative in character, to preserve essential standards by liberalising the situation at the top. In both instances Nietzsche is an important factor. Conrad is a slightly more complicated problem.

'Anarchistic man' – about whom in *Die Gesellschaft* he uses much the same terms as for those imitators of Nietzsche whom he reproaches in *Der Übermensch in der Politik* – may have been distasteful to him, and, while he hit at the power of the state from one point of view, he upheld it from another. All the same, there are features in his argument comparable to those ideas that attracted anarchists to Nietzsche. What the anarchists said about the individual, Conrad said about society, that its individual parts should be allowed to unfold in their individual way. The self-fulfilment of the individual, freed from pressure and restraint, was a fundamental premise of all anarchists and, for all his expressed dislike in *Der Übermensch in der Politik* of anarchic individualism, he was still not as far removed as it might seem from his recently declared belief in the supremacy of the 'freest possible individualism' and the notion that 'all compulsion' is an 'injustice'.[32] One has only to recall in *Der Übermensch in der Politik* the juxtaposing – hardly less than in Schmitt's *Herodes* – of power and freedom to see the point, especially bearing in mind the way in that work power tends to acquire, as with Schmitt, the implication of force, even of violence. Conrad's variations on the theme of *Gewalt* have, in fact, a family likeness to what he had attributed to anarchism in his earlier critique of it, when he described its idea of society as 'ruling by terror (*terrorisierend*)', cramping the 'free awareness of personality'. It is not therefore altogether to be wondered at that Nietzsche continued to attract Conrad despite his criticism of him in *Der Übermensch in der Politik* under the impact of the Subversion Bill.

Thus, the question of power and authority does indeed loom large in all three pamphlets provoked by the bill, but not in a way that enrolls Nietzsche on that score. Schmitt rejects power absolutely. Conrad's target is power at the top. Wolzogen challenges the power on which rest the values of the ruling class as he finds it. Conrad, it is true, expresses anxiety about Nietzsche as an ideological aid to autocracy, but this was not consistent with what he had earlier been saying — and in any case, as much of the evidence in this book will show, this was not how things worked out.

Notes to Chapter VI

[1] Cf. for example, Joachim Steinhagen, *Die Gesetzgebung des Deutschen Reiches zur Bekämpfung politischer Umsturzbestrebungen in den Jahren 1878 bis 1899* (Diss., Schramberg (Schwarzwald), 1935), pp. 40 ff; G. A. Ritter, *Die Arbeiterbewegung im Wilhelminischen Reich* (Berlin, 1959), pp. 25 ff; Gordon A. Craig, *Germany 1866– 1945* (Oxford, 1978), pp. 252 ff.

[2] Cf. *Die Grenzboten* (1895), p. 161.

[3] *Ibid.*, p. 157.

[4] *Neue Preussische Kreuzzeitung* (28 January 1895). The kind of effect attributed to 'subversive' writers, among whom Nietzsche was included, is reflected in the remark of one Centre deputy in the Reichstag that two French anarchists were supposed to have been converted to their cause by reading Ludwig Büchner's *Kraft und Stoff*. Cf. *Stenographische Berichte über die Verhandlungen des deutschen Reichstags*, IX, Legislaturperiode, III. Session, I/1894–5, p. 291.

[5] Cf. *Der Kunstwart* (1895), p. 177.

[6] Cf. Telmann's article 'Literarische Prozesse', in *Die Kritik*, 2 Jg., No. 22 (2 March 1895), pp. 412.

[7] *Die Nation* (1894–5).

[8] The relevant correspondence between Freytag and Hauptmann was printed in *Die Nation* (1894–5), in connection with the petition. This paper took a rather special interest in the Subversion Bill. In the mid-1890s it adopted a markedly friendly attitude to the modernist writers categorised as *die Moderne*, defending them against charges of immorality and anarchism. A liberal paper, it had been founded by Theodor Barth (its editor at the time of the Subversion Bill) and Ludwig Bamberger. The former represented the Freisinnige Vereinigung in the Reichstag for a number of years and the latter too was a liberal deputy.

[9] Letter to Erich Schmidt of 25 February 1895, in Max Cornelius (ed.), *Heinrich von Treitschkes Briefe*, III (Leipzig, 1920), p. 641.

[10] Leipzig, 1895.

[11] *Das Magazin für Litteratur*, 68 Jg., pp. 606–10.

[12] *Friedrich Nietzsche an der Grenze zweier Weltalter* (Leipzig, 1899).

[13] *Der Sozialist* (25 January 1896).

[14] *Werke*, II, p. 801.

[15] Stuttgart, 1895.

[16] *Von Emile Zola bis Gerhart Hauptmann* (Leipzig, 1902), p. 25.

[17] Cf. Krummel, *op. cit.*, pp. 57–8.

[18] *Die Gesellschaft* (1888), pp. 1156ff.

[19] *Ibid.* (1891), p. 1424.

[20] Cf. Conrad's *Wahl-Fahrten: Erinnerungen aus meiner Reichstag-Kandidatenzeit* (1894). Not having been able to trace a copy of this, I am dependent for my knowledge of it on Hedwig Reisinger, *Michael Georg Conrad* (Diss., Würzburg, 1939).

[21] Cf. Dieter Fricke (ed.), *Die bürgerlichen Parteien in Deutschland*, I (Berlin, 1968), p. 638.

[22] Hence his words about 'we small farmers and small craftsmen', constituting 'legions of labour slaves'.

[23] *Die Gesellschaft* (1897), pp. 264–6.

[24] *Ibid.* (1885), pp. 222–3.

[25] 'Aristokratischer Radikalismus: eine Abhandlung über Friedrich Nietzsche', in *Deutsche Rundschau* (1890).

[26] 3rd edition, Berlin, 1906.

[27] Cf. pp. 4, 17, 31, 37, 38, 182, 220, 249.

[28] As Heinrich Stümcke was to point out in his essay 'Aristokratie und Nietzscheanismus', in *Zwischen den Garben* (Leipzig 1899).

[29] Cf. *Wie ich mich ums Leben brachte: Erinnerungen und Erfahrungen* (Brunswick und Hamburg, 1922), p. 197, where Wolzogen mentions how 'Nietzsche's dream of the Superman left its mark on my term Überbrettl'.

[30] *Ibid.*, p. 268.

[31] *Ibid.*, p. 197.

[32] Cf. *Die Sozialdemokratie und die Moderne*, p. 32.

VII

The feminist movement and Nietzsche

Nietzsche said many unflattering things about women and emphasised what would normally be regarded as manly virtues: toughness, power and endurance. So one would not expect him to have been well received in the feminist movement. Women set on improving their lot in society, one might think, would have regarded him more as an enemy than a friend. Some did, but, even then, not because he thought women should have too little freedom, but because he served to encourage some of them to want too much, and of the wrong kind. He aroused strong and passionate feelings. To some women he was the agent of the devil, to others he was a Pied Piper of Hamelin whom, as the champion of selfhood, they were inspired to follow by 'natural instinct to tend and guard *Individualität*'.[1]

The feminist movement, it is important to remember, was divided into two different sectors.[2] One, predominantly proletarian in character, operated in close conjunction with the SPD. The other, organisationally centred on the Allgemeine Deutsche Frauenverein, regarded itself as politically independent. This was an affair essentially of middle-class women, and socialists on the whole viewed it somewhat disdainfully. The women these had in mind were differently placed. Proletarian woman, it was pointed out, spent her day for the most part at a place of work outside the home.[3] This gave her a certain independence, but at the cost of restricting her individuality. Middle-class woman was very much limited to the home, though freed from much of the toil that went with running a house. In the proletarian sector the concern was primarily with women's conditions in the labour market and with social welfare. This was not a preoccupation of the bourgeois sector of the feminist movement, and there the problems were so different that it could be argued from a socialist point of view that it had better go its own way.[4] It was among the bourgeois feminists, moreover, that Nietzsche's influence manifested itself.

To understand how and why, it will be useful first to look at the case of Helene Lange, whose platform was the Allgemeine Deutsche Frauenverein, and who exemplifies certain general characteristics of the feminist movement when Nietzsche burst on the scene.

Helene Lange was a reformer with conservative sympathies. The real conservatism, however, as reflected in the attitude to women's education, was of the sort that had found expression at a conference in Weimar in 1872. The outcome of this amounted to the notion that a woman should above all be so educated that her husband would not be embarrassed by his wife's limitations, bored by her narrow-mindedness, and cramped in the pursuit of higher interests. This was exactly how Lily Braun was brought up. The aim, she said, had been to enable her to provide a nice home atmosphere for her future husband. Helene Lange firmly opposed this attitude, saying that it reflected only the man's point of view and did not correspond to woman's nature. She did think that girls should be taught just by women, but she had only contempt for those who in the conservative interest made a fetish of the idea of a mysteriously precious quality of femininity, reflecting the idea of woman as 'tender, receptive, needing protection, easily influenced, submissive'.[5] The natural characteristics of a woman were important to her, but not to the exclusion of a role in society. Woman, she thought, should be conscious of and confident in her individuality, staking a claim to activity outside the home, and enriching life with qualities derived from her private existence as wife and mother.

If the term 'conservative' is applied to Helene Lange, it can only be in a relative sense. It has to be borne in mind how conservative conservatism was in Wilhelmine Germany, and also that in the circumstances it needed courage to go as far as she did in reformist thinking on the women's question. She can be rather better characterised as liberal up to a point. She greatly respected, for example, the views of the Crown Prince and his consort. His early death, she thought, had dealt the feminist movement, and liberalism itself, a cruel blow,[6] and she was pleased to make contact with a circle of people in Berlin, which she described as including the leading spirits of *Kulturliberalismus*. With them she shared the conviction that change in the social, economic and political situation could only be achieved from within the individual person, through education and *Bildung*. It should not be aimed at in the form of an 'imposed socialistic reordering of society',[7] and she therefore rejected what seemed to her to be the abstract ideas of the so-called 'radicals' in the feminist movement, for whom sex-equality was the primary consideration. Such women, she said, are only concerned to 'fight for something', not to get it 'by growing into it'.[8] She referred here to the trend represented by the Verband Fortschrittlicher Frauenvereine, associated with Anita Augspurg and Wilhelmine Cauer. A good education, in Helene Lange's view, was one that enabled a woman above all to develop her *Individualität* in a civilised and cultured way.

The importance to her of the concept of *Bildung* indicates the tradition from which she came. So too does a comment of hers about the Berlin circle where, she said, people were united 'by common cultural convictions which had grown from the seeds of our classical literature'.[9] The reference is to the eighteenth century when, as embodied in the theory of *Bildung*, Weimar classicism placed the emphasis on a person's ordering of all qualities in the interests of balance, harmony, *Totalität*. When the idea of *Persönlichkeit* was used in this sense in a document handed in to the Prussian Ministry of Education in 1887, Helene Lange was quick to associate herself with it. The idea of *Persönlichkeit*, in its classical context of *Bildung*, involved the notion of selfhood realised through the pursuit of an inward culture, and Helene Lange defined *Bildung* in its authentic classical sense, with Goethe as her model,[10] when she spoke of a 'moulding of the inner life, of the spiritual essence, by receiving impressions from outside which form and shape it': 'In the wider sense we should call a person *gebildet* who has created from within himself what he was able to become'.[11] Applied to feminism, this lent itself, as with Helene Lange, to the idealisation of a type of womanhood characterised by restraint and self-control, by balance and harmony. It was from this point of view that she affirmed the concept of the 'free *Persönlichkeit*' — self-realisation without licence, demanding the 'firm standards of life rooted in the world of the spirit'.[12]

Helene Lange's attitude was on the whole characteristic of the mainstream of the feminist movement in the Wilhelmine period, of which she was one of the most distinguished representatives. Another was her close collaborator Gertrud Bäumer, and she too highlighted as among the 'highest cultural ideals' the concept of 'organically formed *Persönlichkeit*'. The movement, she said, was based above all on the 'right of the free *Persönlichkeit*', which was 'the classical idea of *Individualität*'.[13] The predominantly aesthetic associations of the Weimar tradition of *Bildung* and *Persönlichkeit*, implying the essentially aesthetic criteria of balance and harmony, figure in Gertrud Bäumer's remark about women's 'aesthetic mission'[14] and the home as a 'place of aesthetic culture'[15] as a counter against self-interest and ostentation. For only a woman capable of 'becoming simple enough in character and taste', sufficiently assured 'to throw off the conventional habit of display' and to fight against 'everything puffed up', would, she said, find 'the right personal starting-point for a new culture', one able to 'unfold its joyful creative force only in the element of inner purity and truth'.[16] In Gertrud Bäumer's philosophy of womanhood the 'aesthetic ideals of life' were seen as a corrective to the materialism of modern society. Therefore, incidentally, she praised Nietzsche as one of the 'leading spirits' who realised that the 'struggle for power on the market-place' holds people in thrall and corrupts art and culture.[17]

However, the mainstream of the feminist movement was not by any means as well disposed towards Nietzsche as this reference might suggest. One can begin to see why by considering the values paramount in Helene Lange's philosophy of womanhood in the light of Nietzsche's early series of extra-mural lectures at Basel, *On the Future of our Educational Institutions*, dating from just about the time when, in *The Birth of Tragedy*, he opened up the orgiastic world of the Dionysian.

Particularly relevant in this connection is Nietzsche's condemnation of the German grammar school, with special reference to the importance attached in the curriculum to the so-called German essay. This, Nietzsche said, put a premium on purely formal control, required that all 'excesses' in style, structure and argument should be suppressed, and sacrificed everything 'characteristic and individual' in a young person to a general standard of 'decency'. Nietzsche's criticism of the German essay was related to his scorn, in the same lectures, for the concept of the 'free *Persönlichkeit*'[18] — 'free' in the sense of an idealised spiritual autonomy — which Helene Lange so greatly cherished and Nietzsche here pooh-poohed as abstract and unreal. The general effect, it seemed to him, was to inhibit the life-giving forces in the individual, to neglect a person's dynamic, inner needs, and make a fetish of moderation. Balance, harmony, restraint — virtues of supreme importance to Helene Lange — are thus by implication condemned. The opposite qualities, which she abhorred, she referred to as 'hunger for sensation', the 'passionate intensity (*Erhitztheit*)' of people 'lacking all inner control', 'disarray of instinct' — in short, 'values other than spiritual values'.[19] She saw them coming to the fore in that aspect of the feminist movement known as the New Morality (*Neue Ethik*), and this, with good reason, as we shall see, she blamed on Nietzsche.

The organisational basis of the New Morality was the Bund für Mutterschutz (League for the Protection of Mothers), which came into existence in 1905 on the initiative of Ruth Bré and by 1912 had between three and four thousand members in some nine towns. After disagreement between her and Helene Stöcker, the latter assumed the leadership of the Bund, and it was then that the body of ideas was formulated to which the term 'New Morality' attached itself.

The practical tasks to which the Bund devoted itself need not much concern us. Briefly, its policy revolved around such things as setting up hostels for unmarried mothers, the demand that unformalised marriages should be recognised by the state, advocacy of free love and legalised abortion, easier access to contraception, and the idea of marriage as responsible for prostitution and for the suffering caused by discrimination against unmarried mothers. The New Morality, whose journal was *Die Neue Generation*, argued that marriage, associated as it was with an ascetic moral tradition, no longer satisfied sexual needs, judging by the large numbers of unmarried mothers. Sexual activity was the biological right of all and so should be allowed scope beyond the restraints of marriage. If love in a marriage failed, people should not be forced to stay together in the interests of ethical and legal formalities. The idea of the 'liaison' or *Verhältnis* should be accepted for women, as it was for men, thus doing away with the conventional 'double morality' whereby a man could look for sexual satisfaction elsewhere, but a woman could not. Only on these lines, it was argued, could the needs of people as individuals be provided for and the emancipation of women significantly advanced in ways that mattered most. All this was in line with Nietzsche's principle that to believe in morality is to pass sentence on existence.

The Bund für Mutterschutz itself, in its official statements, was on the whole moderate and responsible, and Heinrich Meyer-Benfey could use *Die Neue Generation* to state that no one is truly free who is merely the slave of passion. Sexual self-control, he said, was important.[20] However, others were inclined to adopt extreme attitudes and to talk wildly about the right and the need to 'live out one's feelings (*sich ausleben*)'. This only encouraged people like Ella Mensch to lampoon the New Morality for its lack of 'notions of restraint',[21] and it helped to make it divisive enough within the feminist movement to put this under strain. But before very long the fortunes of the Bund changed. The crisis came when the general body representing women's organisations (Bund Deutscher Frauenvereine) succeeded in thwarting an attempt to persuade it to adopt a policy of legalised abortion, and in 1909 it refused to admit the Bund für Mutterschutz to membership. When Gertrud Bäumer became president of the Bund Deutscher Frauenvereine, she influenced it in a conservative direction. It was all the more careful then to have nothing to do with the Bund für Mutterschutz, whose further history need not delay us.

Of those who were most active in criticising the New Morality, and who at the same time pointed their finger at Nietzsche as the culprit, the most prominent was Helene Lange. Characteristic was her essay 'Feministische Gedankenanarchie' ('Anarchy in feminist thinking') of 1908,[22] where she turns to ironic effect phrases from its vocabulary such as 'the life-value of love', 'the productive role of passion', 'the dynamic force of eroticism', and pin-points their source in Nietzsche. She felt the need to 'try to save the honour of bourgeois morality', to emphasise not eroticism but the family, the wedding-ring and the marriage ceremony. This was her aim too in 'Die Frauenbewegung und die moderne Ehekritik' ('The women's movement and the modern critique of marriage'),[23] which appeared the following year. It was Nietzsche, she says, who inspired the social and moral 'revaluation of marriage', and she parodies his vocabulary to spice her irony. 'Honest nature against lying convention, uninhibited joy of life against ascetics and obscurantists, the sovereign individual against the banal and intrusive morality of the herd' — who, she asks scornfully, would not respond with enthusiasm to slogans such as these?

Less notable critics of the New Morality included a certain M. Gräfin Münster who was keen to protect youth from its dangers and to warn that 'all the reforming efforts of this new ethics are rooted in Nietzsche's teaching'.[24] Moral greatness, she says, 'can never be achieved in "the living out of *Persönlichkeit*", but only in ... the mastering of human urges and passions'. This is the essence too of a pamphlet by Marie Werner[25] on the theme of the danger of 'immaturity and lack of judgment', with a motto urging readers to 'safeguard your most precious possessions'. One section is prefaced with an appalling quotation from the recently deceased patriotic poet Wilhelm Jordan, obviously chosen because Nietzsche figures as the villain:

Was nach Schopenhauer, Hartmann
    Doch von Lebensmut als Rat blieb,
Was trotz Ibsen und Konsorten
    Noch zur Hälfte wurzelfest blieb:

Von dem Glauben an die Ehre,
    An des Menschen Wert und Pflichten
Lasst ihr Euch vom Truggeist Nietzsche
    Fortbeweisen und vernichten

— the gist of which is that what remained intact after Schopenhauer, Hartmann and Ibsen of 'belief in honour' and the 'value and duties of man', is being allowed to be demolished by the 'deceiver Nietzsche'. 'Revaluation of values', she comments, is now the trendy phrase, 'and there is hardly a single public lecture or large meeting where it does not occur and is not received with rapturous applause.' More responsible and balanced than such rather hysterical comments is Grete Meisel-Hess's book *Das Wesen der Geschlechtlichkeit*, published in 1916. Speaking of the New Morality, she said that there had been a 'period of revaluation', going back to Nietzsche, in the attitude to sexual values. But the process had now gone too far. It had produced a period of 'chaotic effervescence' and, writing in what she calls the mature phase of the movement, she is careful to distance herself from its more extreme manifestations. She is a restrained and on the whole sympathetic witness, but no less insistent on the part played by Nietzsche. He is not, she says, to be blamed for the excesses of the New Morality. People cannot necessarily be held responsible for the use to which their ideas are put, and Nietzsche's ideas have to be understood in a mainly aesthetic sense.

Grete Meisel-Hess's familiarity with the climate of feeling within the New Morality and with the penetration of Nietzsche's influence, comes out in her novel *Die Intellektuellen*,[27] which *Die Neue Generation* reviewed enthusiastically.[28]

The central figure is an educated girl, Olga, who fears that society will have nothing better to offer her than existence as companion in some well-to-do family, and in the Bund für Mutterschutz she finds exactly the contacts she needs. She is not, we are told, the type of woman who wants to go through life alone and serve some alien cause soberly, industriously, with selfless resignation. Rather, as a 'pioneer of those yet to come', she is one of those who, 'strong in instinct and will' (Nietzschean qualities *par excellence*), demand for themselves 'fullness of life', who are not prepared to be fobbed off with the task of looking after other people's children and to be excluded from the 'magic circle' of existence. Her belief is that 'a moment could come which will free the self, now lonely and in bondage, from its ties − and liberate it for ever'. The idea, obviously associated with Nietzsche, is of an emancipating, life-affirming individualism, in protest against the renunciatory attitudes which he so often attacked. Was suffering, Olga wonders, 'to be the world's everlasting heritage?', and her inmost voice told her that 'joy is the soul of the world'. So, she could well have taken as her motto Nietzsche's statement that there is much joy in store 'of which men and women today still have no inkling ... it is something inevitable that we can conjure up in our imagination, if only reason does not stand still'. To recognise this, Nietzsche said, would be the 'greatest progress of all'.[29]

From this point of view, *Die Intellektuellen* invites comparison with Max Zerbst's book *Die Philosophie der Freude* ('The philosophy of joy').[30] Up to a few years previously Zerbst had had close connections with Nietzsche's family and he was a great admirer of his work.[31] Back in 1892 he had defended Nietzsche against Hermann Türcks's attack on him, and some words of his in this connection provided Marie Hecht with the first quotation in her essay about the Nietzsche cult 'in full swing among women today'.[32] Quoting Zerbst, she wrote that 'a great longing came over me for a new god', but not for one who 'dwells among the stars'. It was a longing 'for a fresh, cheerful, earthly god', and 'I found him in Friedrich Nietzsche'.

This more or less defines the central theme of *Die Philosophie der Freude*. 'Every heightening of life', Zerbst writes, clearly thinking of Nietzsche, 'is accompanied by a positive feeling, by a feeling of joy (*Lust*), every hindering of life by a feeling of suffering ....' It is, Zerbst says, here too taking his cue from Nietzsche and often referring to him, 'joy itself as such' that is able to create life. Joy is the 'great liberator and redeemer, alone endlessly creating, re-forming, elevating life' — but suffering 'means compulsion and it binds people in chains'.[33] Zerbst also published the text of two lectures about Nietzsche under the title *Zu Zarathustra*,[34] where he examines the question of love in conjunction with Zarathustra's words about 'becoming what you are'. Love as Nietzsche understands it, says Zerbst, is a rare and special thing, a 'force rooted in the basis of *Persönlichkeit*', the 'holy joy' which man feels when he learns to 'rejoice in his self and in what he creates'. It is the 'deepest and most intimate feeling released in creative man by affirmation of life and affirmation of the self'.[35]

This use of the term *Persönlichkeit* has very different implications from those it had for Helene Lange. She was at pains to stress the contrast between, as one might say, its more Dionysian application and what she herself had in mind. The cultivation of one's 'spiritual individuality', she insisted, was not to be taken 'in the ugly sense which it has nowadays', amounting to no more than 'brutal egoism'. The present time suffered from the 'disease of Nietzscheanism'. It made matters worse by giving this 'cult of the self' attractive names taken from Nietzsche's vocabulary, and she singled out the phrase *sich ausleben* as epitomising what she most disliked.[36]

As used in the New Morality, the term tended to associate selfhood with getting what your instincts want (without the corollary, so important to Nietzsche, of self-mastery and self-overcoming), so it lent itself easily to what can not unfairly be described as vulgarity. This however is a word that one would not want to apply to Helene Stöcker, the most Nietzsche-oriented and most intelligent exponent of this hoped-for ethical revolution.

Born in 1869, she had suffered under the authority of ascetically-minded parents and grew up in a home governed by a calvinistic contempt for the pleasures of the flesh. Dancing and the theatre were seen as sinful, and even *Die Gartenlaube* was regarded with suspicion. Thus her background may well have helped to make her more susceptible to emancipatory ideas about women and, reflected in quotation after quotation in her novel *Liebe*, to the influence of Nietzsche in this connection. It was from Ole Hansen in 1891 that she had first become aware of Nietzsche. From that time on, she said, 'my interest and joy in Nietzsche, and the enrichment I gained from contact with that unique phenomenon among our contemporaries, never ceased'; there was no other mind among them to whom she was so profoundly indebted.[37]

Helene Stöcker's enthusiasm for Nietzsche found expression in a number of essays,[38] the first of which, 'Frauengedanken' ('Thoughts about women'), appeared in 1894. He might have said some unkind things about women, she noted, but no one set on constructing a modern philosophy of one's own or 'striving to absorb the world he lives in can manage without him'.[39] To understand modern life without Nietzsche would be 'like trying to understand the Greeks without Plato'.[40] She expressed gratitude to him for replacing a life-denying, ascetic morality with a 'religion of joy', and for combatting the idea of sexual love as sinful and of woman as impure. He thus liberated people from a sense of guilt and ennobled their love.[41] He recognised that great love is made possible only through the 'richness of the individual as a person', through 'fullness' and 'self-affirmation'. He confronted 'the tired and exhausted', who divide all human qualities into 'good' and 'evil' and so themselves create 'good' and 'evil', with 'feelings that say yes to life'.[42] What women are after, she said, is not just the opportunity to follow a profession, and not merely a little more emotional freedom. They demand a 'new kind of humanity ... Nietzsche's "higher people", who affirm life and affirm themselves' and are characterised by a 'strong and unbroken will to life'. Our conscience commands us, she said, to do what Nietzsche instructed, to 'become what we are'; That is to say, to strive to 'develop all powers latent in us and have the courage to trust ourselves and our womanly nature'. Women must learn to 'prescribe the laws of our own existence, to determine our own scale of values'.[43] It is no wonder that when quoting this, a leading journal could speak of a 'Dionysian dithyramb to woman's future'.[44]

The emphasis here is less on woman's role in society than on the fulfilment of her nature, and this was characteristic of the New Morality in general. This was why it was not particularly interested in the equality of the sexes as an issue, and in turn it made it all the easier for it to sidestep Nietzsche's critical views about women, since these basically arose from the idea that in the nature of things men and women are not equal, and that therefore, as Nietzsche tended to say, a fundamental tension exists between them. This made it less difficult to square enthusiasm for Nietzsche with a general disregard of that notorious remark in *Thus spake Zarathustra* which seemed to suggest, as an item of practical advice, the need to be prepared to whip women. In any case, this remark has nothing to do with women as such, for reasons requiring a separate discussion — they are set forth in the Appendix.

The feminists of the New Morality were however in the habit of quoting some of the statements in the section of *Thus spake Zarathustra* in which that remark occurs, like 'everything about a woman has only one solution, namely pregnancy' and 'the aim is always the child'.[45] Also in *Thus spake Zarathustra* comes the remark 'I never yet found the woman by whom I wanted children except for this woman whom I love ...'.[46]

This is quoted twice in Mathieu Schwann's novel *Liebe*, [47] written in the year of Nietzsche's death and published one year later, in 1901, the intervening part of the novel being a sort of dialogue with Nietzsche-Zarathustra. The book is basically a paeon of praise to 'life': 'I want to dip deep into full, whole undivided life'. 'Truth', 'freedom' and 'joy', we read, can only exist in love; but the present is not the best time for love. [48] If the champions of the New Morality had taken more notice of Schwann's novel they would have rejoiced in such sentiments and also in the reasons given for the obstacles to love in present circumstances — above all, the force of repressive attitudes and institutions, including the prevailing morality of marriage. They would have delighted in the reference to 'life-destroying prudery' as encouraging prostitution, and in the comment that these are issues where 'women themselves must get to work', [49] widening their consciousness and their 'living experience'. Eugen Diederichs, who published Schwann's novel, described it as treating 'the erotic problem in a way pointing towards Nietzsche's idea of raising oneself up through love'. [50] It is a very Nietzschean book in its general attitude and in the Zarathustra-tone of some of its language, and strikingly akin to the mood of the New Morality. Here too, Nietzsche's snootier comments on women did not stand in the way.

They did not create much of a problem either for the novelist Hedwig Dohm, though she did, in passing, ask 'why do you write about women without having anything good to say about them?'. [51] Her story *Werde, die du bist* (1894) gets its title straight from Nietzsche, and it is in his debt in other ways too. *Werde, die du bist* ('Become the woman you are') is about someone who has devoted all her time and energy over a long period to her sick mother. Her parents had never regarded her, being a girl, as an independent person, and so she had no real existence of her own to fall back on when her husband finally died. With nothing to live for and no personal life to build on, she became a quaint old lady, now living in a mental home. Her nature had been 'bound to a chain', she had never had the chance to become a *Persönlichkeit*. 'I had no self', she laments, and, dying, asks herself 'whether perhaps in death my self will be born' and in the beyond 'I shall become what I am'. She had to live as she did, she protests, because she was a woman, and the tablets of the law lay down what sort of life a woman must lead, but 'what is written there is wrong' — so 'let the tablets be destroyed, as Moses destroyed them on Sinai'. [52]

Many touches reflect how Nietzsche helped to inspire this mood of protest. In the mental home she spoke only rarely, but then 'her words breathed an immeasurable melancholy or dithyrambic ecstasy' — the second epithet is the revealing one. She uttered 'deep and sublime thoughts in a form reminiscent of Nietzsche's Zarathustra'.[53] Nietzsche was for her the 'greatest living philosopher' and it is obviously to him that she owes her burning desire to 'transcend things as they are and climb away to greater heights (*hinaus – hinauf*)',[54] to be at least in the end one of those 'wanting to take the upwards path'. 'It is this instinct towards ennoblement', she says, 'that drives me on ....'[55]

Hedwig Dohm's *Werde, die du bist* invites comparison for obvious reasons with the first novel of another highly successful writer, Gabriele Reuter's *Aus guter Familie* ('From a good family') (1895), written before she had any interest in or contact with the feminist movement – it was only while working on it that she began to realise its relevance to her. She then became aware that to get too involved in the movement would distract her from her writing, and that others were more talented in that direction than she.

The central figure of *Aus guter Familie* is a woman driven to mental breakdown by the over-protective existence imposed on her by her parents. A 'flower striving to unfold its nature', she has, too late, the chance to go off with a young man who talks to her about emancipation and urges her not to let herself be dictated to. Does it not attract you, he asks her, to play a part in working for the 'rights of *Persönlichkeit*?'.[56] Another of Gabriele Reuter's novels, *Ellen von der Weiden* (1901), is about a girl from the country with a husband who regards his wife as someone whose main role in life is to support his public image. Looking back, she realises that to have made him happy, 'I should have had to kill the best in myself'. What Christianity calls sin, she reflects, picking up Nietzsche's condemnation of ascetic morality, is a name for everything which 'blossoms in ourselves to highest power and beauty', for experience through which alone 'we become what we are'. God, she says, gave us a nature 'that could not wait', but Christ insists on telling us that this is something that we have to overcome.[57]

Burdened with the task of looking after her widowed mother, Gabriele Reuter found an outlet in literary circles where, amongst others, she met John Henry Mackay, who became a close friend of hers. In a crucial phase of her development around 1890 she abandoned her religious beliefs and lived for a while in the literary *bohème* in Munich. Then she moved with her mother to Weimar, where she joined the Olden circle, to which she read the opening chapter of *Aus guter Familie*, on which all her hopes were now pinned. 'We were all out and out individualists', she recalled about the people she met there, and 'we had the honest belief that we were working in our inmost development'. She and her friends had all read Stirner, who 'had laid the basis for us'. But in the end, she found, he led only into 'grey nothingness', and then Nietzsche 'became our god' and 'around him our minds revolved, like the planets round the sun'. The effect of his work was 'wonderful and intoxicating'.[58]

However, most of those in the New Morality movement who referred so frequently to Nietzsche and used his ideas so liberally did not have the benefit of this kind of preparation, and they were often not of an academic turn of mind anyhow. Where then did they pick up what they knew about him? A major mediator of Nietzsche within the feminist movement was certainly Helene Stöcker, as a writer and as a busily itinerant speaker. She was relatively familiar with Nietzsche whereas many, perhaps the majority, knew about him mainly from gossip. In a sense, the less familiar one was with his work at first hand, the easier it was to bandy about words and phrases which were now so much in the cultural air, such as 'saying yes to life', 'joy', 'revaluation' – typical terms in the vocabulary of the New Morality. The answer to the question is, therefore, that what many knew about Nietzsche was mainly hearsay – if they had read anything at all, it was often only *Thus spake Zarathustra*.

What the protagonists of the New Morality did not properly appreciate was that a programme so fixated, with the help of slogans such as these, on liberating women from sexual restraints could go some way towards accepting man's supremacy. Hedwig Dohm, in fact, accused Laura Marholm of reactionary tendencies because she talked about 'millions of women hearing the silent and unconscious cry, grant us the happiness of being able to live out our woman's nature to the full'.[59] Lily Braun, as concerned as anyone with improving the lot of women, expressed the view that the idea of 'woman true to her "nature as woman"' amounted to the image of woman as 'a "female animal" that merely loves, has children and suckles them'. It was no use imagining that the real problem lay in the handicaps of marriage. Until woman was economically independent the legal bond of marriage was necessary, harsh though its consequences might be in particular cases. 'Only on the basis of economic independence of the sexes one of the other', she wrote, 'will the abolition of the legal form of marriage ... be the key to greater happiness and a higher kind of morality.' She wanted, that is to say, to tackle the problem from an essentially socio-material point of view – and kept Nietzsche out of it.[60]

In short, the way the notion of freeing woman from the limitations of marriage for a fuller sexual life was argued out in the New Morality tended towards an image of woman based essentially on her biological role. From this it was not a very long way towards a distinctly eugenic kind of philosophy, with the emphasis shifted from individual self-realisation to the improvement of the race. The guiding figure was then less Nietzsche than

Darwin, despite the use that Nietzsche had made of the concept of *Zucht* and *Züchtigung*, notably in *The Will to Power* (not published till 1906), with its tribute to the 'great thought of breeding'. The races, he said, 'which cannot bear this idea are doomed; those which feel it is the highest blessing are chosen to be the masters'.[61] But he was talking not so much eugenically as philosophically about the development of 'higher man' and certainly his aim was not to encourage physical conflict between the nations.

Darwin was sometimes mentioned in official statements of the Bund für Mutterschutz, whereas with the New Morality, in so far as it is possible to separate the two, Nietzsche was the name more commonly heard. With an increasing role being played in the Bund by notions recognisably akin to Social Darwinism, Helene Stöcker could say by about 1915 that 'the care for the coming race', is 'the driving force of the Mutterschutz movement'. But it was differently orientated, she added, as compared with Nietzsche. It did not think so much about the creative individual – it was not *genial*. Its perspectives, she said, were social and national.[62]

Ideas on these lines had been developing for some little while in connection both with the Bund and the New Morality. Frequent use of *Auslese* ('selection') and similar terms tended to signal a Social Darwinist direction. In a statement defining the policy of the Bund in 1910, Helene Stöcker said that its aim was to produce a 'new social and sexual order ... in which procreation and parenthood are placed in the service of conscious human selection' in order 'to lead to ever higher stages of development'. It would, she said, tackle 'the problems of higher development through biological and socio-political measures'.[63] By 1897 she had found that she shared 'to a great extent' the Social Darwinist ideas of Alexander Tille; earlier however his championship 'of a different philosophy from her own' had helped to dissuade her from marrying him.[64] In 1911 Max Rosenthal, a leading advocate of the Bund, defined its objectives as not 'individual and ethical', but 'social and ethical'. This substitution points away from Nietzsche. The fact that when Rosenthal spoke of the Bund as aiming at a 'higher development of the human race', it was not Nietzsche but Social Darwinism he was thinking about is reflected in his phrase about 'making the race healthy'. It is mirrored too in his statement that valuable above all was Darwin's idea of development through selection – *Auslese* again – and the survival of the fittest. Nietzsche may sometimes have been a factor, at least in the background, in encouraging Social Darwinist attitudes in the Bund and the New Morality. He probably was, but as we shall see, some Social Darwinists at the time tended to have serious reservations about him. Tempting though it may be, for example, to assume Nietzschean influence behind Rosenthal's statement that 'what is moral is ... what serves and advances the upwards movement of mankind', it is, as the context shows, Darwin to whom he is specifically referring.[65]

The full force of attitudes such as we have been sketching is apparent from Grete Meisel-Hess's article on *Mutterschutz* as a 'social philosophy'.[66] The forms, she wrote regretfully (without reference to Nietzsche, but clearly implicating Darwin), in which motherhood is in the main available to women today, 'guarantees only in a very small number of cases the free development of the process of selection (*Auslese*) by choice of partner in the interests of breeding'. *Mutterschutz* must therefore be given every support because it 'helps the choosing of partners (*Zuchtwahl*) to function naturally as a factor of selection'. It enables it the better to evolve, that is to say, its *auslesendes Wesen*. This means that the sick should be prevented from having children as much as that positive steps should be taken to encourage healthy children. The ultimate implication of Grete Meisel-Hess's argument, motivated amongst other things by anxiety in the Bund für Mutterschutz about decline in the birth-rate, comes in her conclusion 'that the race with the greatest vitality (*Vitalrasse*), the white race, should, as the bearer of the highest culture, spread itself as widely as possible over the earth and not itself be pushed aside by coloured peoples'.

This, of course, was the view of the Alldeutsche Verband, the most important and influential of all the nationalist organisations. It rated Darwin highly and correspondingly despised Nietzsche. Before coming to that part of our discussion however, we have to consider the question of the youth movement, starting with the Wandervogel. The latter's attitude to Nietzsche was negative, which as we shall see, confirms the general picture of where Nietzsche's friends were most likely to be found — least so, that is to say, where strongly *völkisch* or nationalistic values prevailed.

Notes to Chapter VII

[1] Theobald Ziegler, *Die geistigen und sozialen Strömungen Deutschlands im 19. und 20. Jahrhundert* (Berlin, 7th edition, 1921), pp. 510, 531.

[2] For the authoritative work in English on this subject cf. R. J. Evans, *The Feminist Movement in Germany* (London and Beverly Hills, 1976).

[3] Cf. for example, Georg Simmel, 'Der Frauenkongress und die Sozialdemokratie', in *Die Zukunft* (1896), pp. 80 ff.

[4] As with an (unsigned) article 'Bürgerliche und proletarische Frauenbewegung', in *Sozialistische Monatshefte* (1899).

[5] *Lebenserinnerungen* (Berlin, 1921), p. 132.

[6] *Ibid.*, p. 141.

[7] *Ibid.*, p. 136.

[8] *Ibid.*, p. 225.

[9] *Ibid.*, p. 136.

[10] Cf. Helene Lange's *Weltanschauung und Frauenbewegung* (Berlin, 1900) (p. 8), where she instances his lines:

> Sofort nun wende dich nach innen,
> Das Centrum findest du da drinnen ...

[11] 'Bildungsfragen', in *Die Frau* (October 1898).

[12] *Lebenserinnerungen*, p. 292.

[13] *Die Frau und das geistige Leben* (Leipzig, 1911), p. 79.

[14] *Ibid.*, p. 321.

[15] *Ibid.*, p. 315.

[16] *Ibid.*, p. 323.

[17] *Ibid.*, p. 299.

[18] *Werke*, III, pp. 203 ff.

[19] *Lebenserinnerungen*, p. 123.

[20] 'Die neue Ethik und ihre Gegner', in *Die Neue Generation* (1908), pp. 153 ff. Cf. also his article 'Zur Verständigung über die "neue Ethik"', in *Die Frau* (1907–8), pp. 297 ff.

[21] Ella Mensch, *Bildungsstürmer in der Berliner Frauenbewegung*, (3rd ed. n.d.), [ca 1905], p. 9.

[22] *Neue Rundschau* (1908). Reprinted in Helene Lange's *Kampfzeiten: Aufsätze und Reden aus vier Jahrhunderten* II, (Berlin, 1928), pp. 1 ff.

[23] *Ibid.*, pp. 8 ff.

[24] Cf. 'Wie bewahren wir die Jugend vor den Gefahren der neuen Ethik?', in Paula Müller (ed.), *Die 'Neue Ethik' und ihre Gefahr* (Lichterfelde-Berlin, 1908).

[25] *Die Grüne Gefahr* (Hagen i.W., n. d.).

[26] The poem was published in the Munich *Allgemeine Zeitung* of 7 September 1893. Nietzsche figures as a 'deceiver' because Jordan goes on to accuse him of having pinched material from his own work without acknowledgment.

[27] Berlin, 1911.

[28] No. 11 (1911), pp. 487–8.

[29] *Werke*, I, p. 948.

[30] Leipzig, n. d. [1904].

[31] Cf. C. P. Janz, *Nietzsche*, II (Munich and Vienna, 1979), p. 175.

[32] *Die Frau*, 6 Jg. (1898–9), pp. 486 ff.

[33] pp. 147 ff.

[34] Leipzig, n. d., [1905].

[35] pp. 78–9.

[36] Cf. 'Bildungsfragen'.

[37] From her unpublished autobiography ('Lebensabriss'), dictated by her in 1939 and held, in typescript, in the Swarthmore College Peace Collection, Swarthmore, Pennsylvania. I owe my knowledge of its existence to Professor R. J. Evans, who most kindly put a copy of the relevant sections at my disposal. Its chaotic pagination makes page references virtually impossible.

[38] Some of them are reprinted in her *Die Liebe und die Frauen* (Minden i. W., n. d.).

[39] 'Friedrich Nietzsche und die Frauen', in *Das Magazin für Litteratur* (12 and 15 February 1898).

[40] 'Zur Nietzsche-Lektüre', in *Der Volkserzieher* (6 and 13 November 1898).

[41] Quoted in Evans, *op. cit.*, p. 119.

[42] 'Der Wille zur Macht', in *Jugend* Bd. 1, No. 18, (1903), pp. 306 ff.

[43] 'Unsere Umwertung der Werte' (1897), in *Die Liebe und die Frauen*, pp. 6 ff.

[44] *Neue Deutsche Rundschau/Freie Bühne* (1899), p. 107.

[45] *Werke*, II, pp. 328–30.

[46] *Ibid.*, II, p. 475. The apparent simplicity of the message however is spoilt by what Schwann omits, namely, the identification of the woman with 'eternity'.

[47] pp. 185, 202.

[48] p. 13.

[49] p. 103.

[50] 'Lebenslauf: Skizze zu einer Selbstbiographie', written 1920–1 and never published. I was very kindly allowed access to it in the archives of the Diederichs Verlag.

[51] 'Nietzsche und die Frauen', in *Die Zukunft* (1898).

[52] *Wie Frauen werden – Werde, die du bist* (Breslau, 1894). Facsimile edition of these two stories. (Frankfurt am Main. n. d.), pp. 176, 192, 193, 207, 236.

[53] *Ibid.*, p. 151.

[54] *Ibid.*, pp. 224, 234.

[55] *Ibid.*, p. 201.

[56] 27th and 28th edition (Berlin, 1931), pp. 307, 354.

[57] Fischer edition ('Fischers Bibliothek zeitgenössischer Romane') (Berlin, n. d.), p. 129.

[58] *Vom Kinde zum Menschen: Geschichte meiner Jugend* (Berlin, 1921), pp. 448, 449.

[59] 'Reaktion in der Frauenbewegung', in *Die Zukunft* (1899), pp. 279 ff.

[60] 'Ellen Key und die Frauenbewegung', in *ibid.*, pp. 318 ff. For Helene Stöcker's comments on this article cf. 'Lily Braun und die Frauenfrage', in *Das Magazin für Litteratur* (1899).

[61] *Werke*, III, p. 437.

[62] *Zehn Jahre Mutterschutz* (Berlin, n. d.).

[63] 'An unsere Leser', in *Die Neue Generation* (1910).

[64] 'Lebensabriss'. Cf. note 37.

[65] 'Ziele und Bestrebungen des "Deutschen Bundes für Mutterschutz"', in *Die Neue Generation* (1911), p. 161.

[66] 'Mutterschutz als soziale Weltanschauung', in *ibid.* (1911), pp. 150 ff.

VIII

The Youth Movement and Nietzsche

Nietzsche expressed some very outspoken criticism of the German educational system and pinned high hopes on young people themselves as the agents of reform. The Wandervogel arose just before the turn of the century, as a protest against the same features of society with which Nietzsche had found fault, and held that youth should take the initiative in creating a way of life of its own. This might lead one to expect Nietzsche to have been an inspiration in the creation of the Wandervogel movement and to have met with a very positive response in Wandervogel circles. This, however, was not the case. Rather later, in a different sector of the Youth Movement, Nietzsche did come into his own. This was when, just before the war, the Free German Youth (*Freideutsche Jugend*) was founded, sharing in some respects the ideals of the Wandervogel, but diverging from it in others. Here, by contrast with the Wandervogel, Nietzsche was as we shall see, a very significant influence.

The decisive part of Nietzsche's criticism of education is to be found in the second of his *Untimely Meditations* in which, twenty-five years or so before the beginning of the Wandervogel movement, he set forth his views on the failings of education and its reform. Education merely imparted knowledge, he said. It had nothing to do with 'life', and deadened the vital springs of existence. But to be directly in touch with 'life' was what young people yearned for. They wanted to experience it, not just to learn about it. He insisted that this was something that they could win for themselves and it was by virtue of their youth that they could do so. 'Release this', Nietzsche urged, 'and at the same time you will have liberated "life".'[1] Then, and only then, would come about the 'kingdom of youth'.[2] What phrase could better describe what the Wandervogel was after?

Moreover, the ideas of certain writers of the time could also point towards a connection between Nietzsche and the Wandervogel.

One such writer was the Protestant theologian Albert Kalthoff, a pastor in Bremen from 1898, author in 1900 of *Friedrich Nietzsche und die Kulturprobleme unserer Zeit* ('Friedrich Nietzsche and the cultural problems of our time') and five years later of *Religion der Modernen* ('The religion of modern man'). Another, likewise a Protestant clergyman, was Arthur Bonus, whose *Vom Kulturwert der deutschen Schule* ('On the cultural value of the German school') appeared in 1904.

In the first of his two books[3] Kalthoff says that he is one of those for whom Nietzsche's importance lies less in what he affirms than in his 'negations'. He is against anything that leads to an 'impoverishment of human nature' and limits or destroys *Persönlichkeit*, he is for whatever facilitates the full 'shaping of the individual life'. Kalthoff's own idea of the future amounts to a paraphrase of some of Nietzsche's basic views: 'less and less the deadness of the mass, less and less the instinct of the herd ... ever richer individuation, more and more ... the unfolding of *Persönlichkeit*'.[4]

The chapter on Nietzsche in the second of these books accordingly recommends his ideas as particularly applicable to the needs of youth.[5] His teaching, Kalthoff says, is a 'message of rejoicing for all young hearts who ... find pleasure in casting away the rusty chains that bind them and in destroying crumbling altars'. Following Nietzsche, it should be a delight to young people now 'to create the new values of life' and, instead of the 'torturing command "thou shalt"', which murders *Persönlichkeit*, to liberate this by bravely proclaiming "I will"'. Kalthoff wishes, therefore, to impart to German youth the idea of Nietzsche as their 'educator', from whom they can learn how 'to form the higher man', how to become the Superman – or, as he prefers to say, the 'God man'. By this he understands a person for whom 'there is no necessity blindly ruling over him and governing him as if he had no will of his own', who recognises 'only what he himself does', and 'makes all necessity into the power of his own will'. No one, Kalthoff argues, ever experienced more deeply and interpreted more significantly than Nietzsche youth's 'hunger and thirst for life', its craving for 'union with the earth' and its yearning 'lovingly to surrender itself to all reality'. 'All young hearts turn rejoicingly' to such a man. Elsewhere too Kalthoff sings Nietzsche's praises – in his *Zarathustras Predigten* ('The sermons of Zarathustra'),[6] for example, where he figures as 'our leader', the 'prophet of a new age', who 'as no other man incorporates the sufferings and joys of our age, its disease, and its way to recovery'.[7]

As to Bonus, he had some reservations about Nietzsche.[8] But what Eugen Diederichs called his interest in 'full, strong life',[9] evident in his *Religion als Schöpfung* and particularly in *Vom neuen Mythos*,[10] suggests, at least from this point of view, an obvious affinity. Man, says Bonus, wants 'broad, full, intensive, unlimited life', and a major hindrance to this, in his view, is education. *Vom Kulturwert der deutschen*. which Bonus saw as a continuation of *Religion als Schöpfung*,[11] fits into this general context easily enough. Its concern, strikingly reminiscent of Nietzsche and almost certainly in his debt, is to release what is potentially creative in the child. Therefore, it argues, the amount that children have to learn should be radically cut down and the role of the school drastically reduced. The aim would be to set free the creative impulse and enable it to flourish, as Nietzsche had demanded.

With notions of this kind in the air, it is not surprising to find people taking Nietzsche for granted as an important factor behind the Wandervogel, with German youth, it was even said, shaken by the 'paroxysms of the Nietzsche fever'.[12] But it is by no means so certain that young people did bother all that much about Nietzsche. There will have been some who raved about *Thus spake Zarathustra*,[13] but by and large, as far as one can now judge, most young people were not particularly interested in him, and knew little, or more usually nothing, about him. Walter Hammer could speak of Wandervogel youth 'storming forward in the direction to which Nietzsche pointed' and about the Wandervogel having 'achieved Nietzsche's new educational ideals'[14] — though this need imply no more than identity of purpose. Some statements went further than this, like the remark that Nietzsche was among 'the most significant of the contemporaries of the Wandervogel from whom it derived its inner content', and whose magic spell 'summoned youth to new areas of struggle', where it was 'to take to itself the right to establish new values'.[15]

The decisive influence however, as all the evidence clearly shows, did not come from Nietzsche, but from Julius Langbehn, author of *Rembrandt als Erzieher*, and from Paul de Lagarde. In Werner Kindt's handbook of the Youth Movement, for example, Nietzsche is listed in the short biographies of people of the older generation who influenced the Youth Movement in general.[16] But in the volume dealing more specifically with the Wandervogel he does not figure in any of the texts.

It was certainly not anything that he knew about Nietzsche that led Karl Fischer, a sixth-former in the grammar school in Steglitz, to found the Wandervogel at the turn of the century — in the first instance by the devious means of using a shorthand class as a hiking club and, in order to give it a cover of respectability, placing it under the auspices of local worthies in the form of the Committee for the Organisation of School Excursions.

Steglitz, in the western part of Berlin and still untouched by industry, was a favoured residential area. People living there were, as one might expect, strongly traditionalist, viewing the aim of education as to prepare young people to fit into their conservative world and to safeguard its values in the future. The headmaster of the grammar school was, we are told, a 'reactionary of the most extreme kind', who — as one might expect — viewed Nietzsche with horror, without apparently ever having read a word he had written.[17] In the school itself, it is true, Nietzsche was not unknown, as one can see from an account of life in the sixth form at this time.[18] There was a circle of pupils where he was sometimes discussed, but it had nothing to do with the setting up of the Wandervogel. Karl Fischer seems to have shared his headmaster's ignorance of Nietzsche. It was said that he followed Nietzsche's ideas, but this could not apply to his intentions and, like Hammer's remarks, could only refer to very general resemblances. Like Nietzsche, he certainly took a poor view of what went on in school in the name of education and wanted to do something about it in the interest of pupils as individuals.

Indifferent as he was to Nietzsche, Fischer hero-worshipped Lagarde.[19] A favourite quotation of his, often used in the Wandervogel, was where Lagarde expressed the hope for 'conspirators among us', working 'for the great tomorrow', 'Many a German', Fischer once said, 'recognised in these words ... his own heart's desire', sharing the sense of bitterness which inspired this utterance of 'that perceptive and lonely man'.[20] Fischer was equally keen on Julius Langbehn. He made a point of reading extracts from *Rembrandt als Erzieher* to those he took with him on Wandervogel expeditions, and would address his followers as 'you Rembrandt Germans'.[21] 'The longing for free, spiritual man', it was stated, 'is what we Wandervögel share with the Rembrandt German' – a common way of referring to Langbehn. There is a 'spiritual relationship between him and the ultimate purpose of our Wandervogel existence, which is to become true people'.[22] It has been said, with reference both to Lagarde and Langbehn, that the Wandervogel 'became the main offshoot of their neo-romanticism'.[23]

The appeal of these two writers to Fischer was symptomatic of his allegiance to the *völkisch* movement, in which both played so important an ideological part. In founding the Wandervogel, his desire had been 'consciously to influence the history of the Fatherland' and 'in particular he wanted to kindle in them an interest in the eastern border regions and arouse in them a longing for the possession of colonies'.[24] It was not by chance that the hiking Wandervögel made a point of exploring the frontier areas. Twenty-five years ago, Fischer was to write, as schoolboys 'we lived the struggles of our *Volkstum*'. This was the reason for the Wandervogel excursions, beginning in 1903, to the Bohemian Forest. Thereafter 'trips to the frontiers' were 'a matter of duty and honour for every person enrolled in the movement ...'.[25] The preface to the 1915 re-issue of the *Zupfgeigenhansl*, the Wandervogel songbook, declares the need for people to become 'more and more German'. Therefore, it says (making a transitive verb out of the intransitive *wandern*), 'take possession for yourself of what is German by walking over it (*erwandert Euch, was deutsch ist*)'.

Fischer could thus be described as a '*volkhafter* revolutionary',[26] and he was a rather autocratic one too, fond of exercising authority. This side of his character was much commented on by those who knew him, and it stamped itself on the structure of the Wandervogel. Fischer organised this on a strictly hierarchical basis, with himself at the top as *Oberbachant* and under him, in descending order, *Bachanten, Burschen* and *Scholaren*. Admission, in a ritualised ceremony, required an oath of loyalty to Fischer as *Oberbachant*. His attitude, in fact, was too assertive for some people's taste, and the unity of the movement suffered. *Völkisch* characteristics, however, were a pretty constant factor, reflected in the popularity in Wandervogel circles of novels like Heinrich Sohnrey's *Das fremde Blut* ('Alien blood') and Hermann Burte's *Weltfeber*. Fischer was very friendly with Sohnrey, who was a member of his committee, and also with Ludwig Gurlitt, a teacher at his school who was well disposed towards the Wandervogel.[27]

Gurlitt's *Der Deutsche und sein Vaterland* ('The German and his fatherland'),[28] which was a considerable success in nationalist circles, was a book that Fischer much admired. Its basic philosophy was that children must be allowed to develop in accordance with their inner nature, an idea which he championed also in other books and articles. Educational systems, he complained, never see the single person as a whole, indivisible personality, but always start from preconceived ideas and opinions, to which the pupil has to subordinate himself'.[29]

This may sound rather like Nietzsche, but Nietzsche has no part in that book. Gurlitt's heroes are of a different kind. They include above all Lagarde, whose *Deutsche Schriften* Gurlitt thought particularly important, and also the ultra-nationalistic Houston Stewart Chamberlain, whose work he much respected as embodying the spiritual legacy of Langbehn. In one article,[30] explaining why he disliked educational systems and wanted to see the role of the school reduced, he pleaded the need for German youth to be enabled to live 'in happiness and joy'. There may possibly be a trace of Nietzsche in this, but the reason why Gurlitt wanted pupils above all to enjoy themselves is the wholly un-Nietzschean one that they would then the better love their country and be more naturally inclined to think and act patriotically. The article in part recapitulates the gist of a recent conference on education where, Gurlitt notes with approval, stress on the need for healthy children was coupled with the demand for 'joyful learning (*fröhliche Wissenschaft*), for liberation from alien ... methods of teaching', in short, 'for a truly German type of education, aiming at the free unfolding of *Persönlichkeit*'.

This quotation, with its echo of one of Nietzsche's titles, but expressing thoughts that Nietzsche would not have tolerated, is symptomatic of Gurlitt's general attitude. It is notable too for the double application of the notion of selfhood, to the individual and to the *Volk*. We find this in Fischer likewise.

How, he asked, worried about the effects of modern industrial society, 'can we, as a *Volk* ... become ourselves?'[31] Gurlitt's mention of the need to keep out what is alien suggests the answer implied in Fischer's question. In the light of that one can more easily understand the anti-semitic strain in the Wandervogel, exemplified particularly in its journal *Führerzeitung*. For the stress in the *völkisch* movement on selfhood, extended from individual to *Volk*, lent itself to the thesis that the *Volk*, being a *Persönlichkeit* with an *Individualität* of its own, could not without corrupting its essence absorb alien elements. 'Alien blood', we remember, was the title of a novel popular with the Wandervogel.

Youth too, it was said, had an integrity of its own which it was important to cherish and preserve. One way of doing this was to counter the intrusive effect of urban existence. This, as one much respected Wandervogel figure stressed, was the 'great propagandistic idea' behind the movement. City life, he said, 'corrupts youth', 'distorts its instincts', and 'alienates it more and more from a natural, harmonious way of life'. 'Redeem yourself', was his call, 'wander through the countryside, and there seek the person you have lost, plain, simple, natural man'.[32]

So, when Kurt Gerlach's book *Germantik* — archaically sub-titled 'The book of the true life, a German book' — appeared in 1914, the *Führerzeitung* recommended it as 'the very thing for our young people'. The first of a planned series of 'books about the freshness of life (*Bücher vom frischen Leben*)', it was aimed, in the words of one advertisement, at 'German boys and girls struggling to find a way out of the narrowness and decay of our time, which has lost its direction'. It is the story of a young man who on his travels discovers much that is 'hollow and false', and meets people who embody the general decadence. This country, we read, was once full of 'freshness and vitality'. Now people lack all 'strength and certainty'. Himself brought up in a town, he is on the look-out for just such qualities, and, with his friend, finds them in a Wandervogel group whom they encounter on their travels. They recognise that these are the people 'that will one day be the truly German essence, rising ever higher'.[33]

The Wandervogel, serving here as a model for the rejection of what is artificial and corrupt in society and showing how to recover a natural way of life, thus lends itself to association with the movement for *Lebensreform* ('reform of life'). The ramifications of this included the setting up of rural colonies, the cult of nudism, vegetarianism and, rigorously insisted on in the Wandervogel, the tabooing of alchohol and nicotine. The purpose of the movement was to restore man to a kind of existence where he would be more fully himself by being closer to nature. Life-reform, one was told, meant self-reform. One article in the *Lebensreform* journal was about man's need to attain his 'true self'. Its point of reference was theosophy and oriental philosophy,[34] illustrating the fact that, after all we have been saying about Nietzsche and the theme of selfhood, it was always necessarily Nietzsche who prompted it. In the *völkisch* context, Langbehn and Lagarde were more commonly the inspiration.

Lebensreform and Wandervogel joined hands in the person of Walter Hammer who enrolled Nietzsche in the service of *Lebensreform* and wrote a book on the subject — not a very illuminating one, and it hardly lives up to the promise of its title.[35] What *Lebensreform* meant to Hammer is explained by his statement that its adherents were 'champions of a new culture' who 'adopt a negative attitude to the machine age in Western Europe'. They seek to 'simplify life' as a way of liberation 'from the chains of today's predominantly materialistic form of existence', thus aiming at the 'strengthening of *Persönlichkeit*'.[36]

Hammer was attracted to Nietzsche not merely because he could use him, as someone known to have experimented with a meat-free diet,[37] to advance the cause of health foods and fresh air. His interest in Nietzsche went deeper than that, marking a change from the negative role that he has so far had to play in this chapter. Hammer held office in the Wandervogel, and it is all the more striking that, while doing so, he got as far as writing a short, simple, but mainly positive book about Nietzsche, designed to popularise his ideas.

Its title *Nietzsche als Erzieher* ('Nietzsche as educator'), like that of a number of books at this time, was modelled on Langbehn's *Rembrandt als Erzieher*. Its publication was around the time of the outbreak of war. So it was courageous on Hammer's part to stress to the extent that he did the idea of Nietzsche as the 'good European'[38] and to use him to criticise what Hammer regards as objectionable features in his fellow countrymen. His (and Nietzsche's) advice to them is 'remember you are a German — and degermanise yourself (*entdeutsche Dich*)'[39] — a dig perhaps at the Alldeutsche Verband whose journal was always prefaced on its title-page with the first part of this quotation.

So Hammer had many good things to say about Nietzsche and he made an honest attempt to provide a simple account of his thought. All the same, he did not regard him as suitable reading within the Wandervogel. Nietzsche and the Wandervogel seem rather to be alternatives from the way he talks about them. If, he says, you are not yet a member of the Wandervogel, 'lay your copy of *Thus spake Zarathustra* aside and join it'.[40] Younger members of the Wandervogel, he thought, should steer clear of Nietsche. It is to those who 'have passed through the school of the Wandervogel' that he addresses

himself in his book.[41] By this time the young Wandervogel will have developed
an attitude of his own, will be 'independent and strong in character'.

Even so, *Nietzsche als Erzieher* got a cool reception in some Wandervogel
circles, and Hammer received a dusty answer when he wrote to *Der Vortrupp*,
a Wandervogel paper, to try to interest it in his book, presumably in the
hope of having it reviewed. It wasn't a simple matter, he was told by Hans
Paasche, one of the editors, and needed thinking about. The important
thing, it was added, was not to expose the movement to 'misunderstandings',
and it was in everyone's interest 'not to push ourselves forward in a one-
sided way before we are an invincible force'.[42] The misgivings were obviously
from the point of view of the attention that Hammer gave to Nietzsche's
anti-German and anti-nationalist opinions. *Der Vortrupp* described itself as
a journal devoted to *Deutschtum* and another of its editors was Hermann
Popert, author of the *völkisch* (and *Lebensreform*) novel *Helmut Harringa*.
The *Führerzeitung* referred to Hammer's book as 'dangerous poison for
young people'. It was best, it thought, to keep at a distance the work of
this 'dark, lonely, sick and ultimately mad philosopher' and to avoid his
'wild landscape' beyond good and evil.[43] Criticism of the book is also reflected in a circular[44] which Hammer addressed in November 1914 'to the
heroes of the right and left banks of the Rhine in so far as they have felt
called to sit in judgment over me'. They had been told, he supposes, that in
his book on Nietzsche he had singled out the faults of Germans for attack,
and Germans would indeed, he adds, be very wrong to assume complacently
that they were models of perfection. To be improved, they needed to be
criticised. Another circular,[45] dated 1915, reveals that the Wandervogel
organisation of the Lower Rhine had gone so far as to expel Hammer from
membership. The reason, he imagines, was his scornful attitude in his Nietzsche book to what he regarded as the more philistine aspects of the German
mentality and the fact that he was sympathetic towards Nietzsche's critical
views about religion.

The chilly reception accorded to Hammer's book within the Wandervogel
movement might seem to be at odds with the idea which became quite wide-
spread, that German soldiers went to war in 1914 with Nietzsche in their
hearts and *Thus spake Zarathustra* in their kitbags. This is at least very
doubtful, as Oscar Levy hastened to point out as soon as the war was over.[46]
It was, he said, 'one of the rarer items' that German soldiers had taken with
them. It is hard to prove him wrong, whether with regard to soldiers in
general or ex-Wandervogel soldiers in particular; naturally, the evidence is
elusive. There was, it is true, a special edition for the troops, and it was
stated in 1916 that *Thus spake Zarathustra* was among the books 'now being

most widely read at the front' — but with the comment that this was a claim made by admirers of Nietzsche.[47] A correspondent in the nationalistic *Deutsche Lehrer-Zeitung*,[48] interested in what the troops were reading, reported in 1918 that he had noticed one soldier reading *Thus spake Zarathustra* and another a book by Wilhelm Bölsche, but without any suggestion that the one was any more typical than the other.

One consideration in particular should lead us to take with a pinch of salt the rumour that there were lots of copies of *Thus spake Zarathustra* being avidly read in the trenches. This is the part played in encouraging it by that popular, obnoxious and perversely beautiful story by Walter Flex, *Der Wanderer zwischen beiden Welten*, published in 1916. It is fiction in more senses than one. For in real life Ernst Wurche, the ex-Wandervogel hero of the story, on whom the idealisation of the Wandervogel depends, had had only relatively slight links with the Wandervogel, though in the story he is supposed to have been deeply involved in the movement. He had had no contact with it while at school, nor as a theology student at Halle. It was only when he went to Berlin that his short-lived connections with it began. He never even took part in a major Wandervogel trip — he was getting ready for one when war broke out.[49] If, however, as the story intends, we are to take his association with the Wandervogel seriously, this does not do the movement much good.

Wurche admired in *Thus spake Zarathustra* above all the uplifting thought that man was 'something to be overcome'. The challenge of war and confrontation with death give Wurche the chance to realise this idea in his own person, but his response to it does him little credit. He goes about destroying things and people rather as someone merely relishing yet again the beauties of the countryside. War for him is just an opportunity to 'experience' life to the full — *Erlebnis* is among his most characteristic concepts. He had always looked forward to 'experiencing' an assault as a sort of culmination, and the thought of it fills him with delight.

Death is for him just another and intenser form of 'experience'; for 'great souls' it is the 'greatest experience of all'. He goes about his business rather in the manner of an artist with his material. When he has to hand over his platoon on being transferred, he feels 'like an artist who has to let others continue the work he has begun'. War is sublimated, and Wurche himself is given the image — which photographs of him as a rather insignificant-looking youth hardly confirm — of a natural and ennobling grace. Death is made to seem beautiful and killing all the more splendid for being what God intended: 'life, as it grows old, should rejuvenate itself from the eternal youth of death according to God's will'. Flex applies this idea to Germany too in his comment about the 'eternal German *Volk*' as a 'moral belief' which, 'as Ernst Wurche would have said, can be realised in the heroic death of a people'.[50] In the Wandervogel it was claimed for young people that they should be encouraged to develop as nature intended and in Flex's story the notion of the Wandervogel as 'the struggle of German youth for its right to grow in its natural way' interplays with the concept of Germany itself unfolding in war its inherent individual essence, its *Persönlichkeit*, in the service of the 'world-redeeming mission of *Deutschtum*'.

In short, one could hardly wish for a better confirmation than *Der Wanderer zwischen beiden Welten* of the Wandervogel's false romanticism and its *völkisch* nationalism. One can all the better understand how it was that models such as Langbehn and Lagarde suited its purposes better than Nietzsche.

If Nietzsche had a very minor place in the Wandervogel movement, he had an important one in the philosophy of Gustav Wyneken, the leading figure in the Freideutsche Jugend,[51] and with this we come to the other main aspect of the Youth Movement in Wilhelmine Germany. Nietzsche was as significant for the Freideutsche Jugend as he was negligible in the case of the Wandervogel. It was only with the advent of the Freideutsche Jugend, as Walter Laqueur said,[52] that Nietzsche entered the Youth Movement. 'Where did today's Youth Movement actually come from?', Eugen Diederichs asked in 1918, referring to the Freideutsche Jugend, and he answered that 'the spark that set it off was without a doubt Nietzsche's prophecy of the Superman', meaning his concentration on things of this world, his *Diesseitsgefühl*. This, he said, together with his longing for man's self-redemption, 'inspired the ethos of the new man, rather as Rousseau, a century earlier, redeemed mankind from the Enlightenment.[53]

However, it was not so much the young people themselves who brought Nietzsche in as their leaders. 'It is less a question of what the young actually said', Diederichs remarked about the ideas prevalent in the Freideutsche Jugend, 'than of a whole attitude to life which the older generation could express better.'[54] He was one of those instrumental in bringing about the inaugural meeting of the Freideutsche Jugend in 1913, and he could describe himself as godfather to the Youth Movement. Likewise, Wilhelm Flitner was referring specifically to the Freideutsche Jugend when he said that Diederichs 'helped to release the forces at work in it',[55] and another writer stated that 'one cannot think of the Youth Movement ... without the influence of Eugen Diederichs'.[56] 'Loyalty to oneself as the basis, boldness in exercising one's will in shaping one's own self, and action as the synthesis of both'[57] – this was how Diederichs defined the governing concept, and it was in this spirit that the famous resolution on the Hohe Meissner talked of the right of German youth to mould its own life in its own way. Language such as this helps to explain how Diederichs could say that the decisive spark which kindled the Freideutsche Jugend was Nietzsche's 'longing for self-salvation'.[58] Nietzsche's idea of *Persönlichkeit*, Diederichs had remarked in 1904, was a decisive factor in his own development.[59] Now he was helping to see to it that Nietzsche should leave his mark on the Youth Movement.

Nietzsche would have welcomed the remark in the speeches on the Hohe Meissner that 'everyone should feel akin to us who takes the problem of his self seriously'.[60] The last thing that he would have wanted to hear however was the sort of remarks made by Gottfried Traub, at the time a pastor, and later better known as a notorious Deutschnationaler. It was left to Wyneken to warn passionately against chauvinistic talk of this kind. Has it really come to this, he asked, that one 'only has to dish up a few words from the nationalist vocabulary and go on about *Deutschtum* to get applause and shouts of bravo?'. He was for international values and he praised those who in the past had subordinated their own country to the welfare of mankind. All nations now faced the same problems, and it would be better to set about tackling these than to fight about territorial possessions. We live, he added, in difficult times, and so 'we do right to declare our support for the words of that great thinker: "A happy life is not our lot, but rather, and this is the highest thing a man can ask for, an heroic one" '.[61]

These are Schopenhauer's words, but it is more than likely that Wyneken took them from Nietzsche, who singles them out in the third of the *Untimely Meditations*.[62] Wyneken went on to tell his audience to be 'keen to learn', 'not to take the easy way', and to accept as their master him 'who demands the highest of them and views them as worthy of being told the most severe truth', to be people endowed with the 'spirit of obedience' and with that 'inner discipline without which the armies of the spirit are like chaff in the wind'. This is wholly, and surely consciously, in the mood of Nietzsche's tribute to Schopenhauer in that essay, and of the section in *Thus spake Zarathustra* where Zarathustra, summoning those he is addressing to have the courage to be warriors in the service of understanding (*Erkenntnis*), calls on them to face the dangers that its service demands and to grasp what this means in terms of commanding and obeying: 'Let your excellence (*Vornehmheit*) be your power to obey; when you give orders, let this be an act of obedience'.[63]

Wyneken was subject to so many influences that he has been criticised for being too eclectic[64] — it would be fairer to commend him, by contrast with the Wandervogel, for being open to intellectual stimuli. There were various strands in his thinking, and important among them is one that links Fichte and Nietzsche.[65] His position with regard to both was complicated. We should understand it dialectically in much the same terms as the relationship of Wyneken's *Freie Schulgemeinde*, the concept which he realised in his famous school at Wickersdorf, to the Wandervogel. The latter bypassed the school as institution, the former set out to work through it, changing it in the process. The *Freie Schulgemeinde*, as Wyneken saw it, was a sort of synthesis of Wandervogel and school, on a higher level. Likewise, Fichte and Nietzsche were for him opposite but complementary figures. Nietzsche, Wyneken wrote, 'affirms life which rises up from below', Fichte affirms 'intellectuality (*das Geistige*) which comes from above'. The school, in Wyneken's conception, had to respect the natural needs of youth — life, as it were, rising from below — but at the same time it had to function as the 'intermediary of mind'.[66]

It was above all the intellectual dimension that Wyneken found wanting in the Wandervogel which, he said in the same context, ran the risk of sacrificing 'culture in favour of youth'. For its part, the Wandervogel saw the Freideutsche Jugend as destroying the world of youth which it had created and so as 'an attempt to institute a new world by intellectual means', something which from its point of view 'could only spring from the depths'.[67] Diederichs too, despite the very good relations he had established with the Wandervogel, especially at Jena, came to have serious reservations about it, for much the same reasons as Wyneken. When, for example, in 1916 he was approached about the publication of a Wandervogel journal, he reacted cautiously. Its level, he said, would have to be more than just 'emotional'. It would have to set aside the usual 'Wandervogel chatter' and tackle seriously problems of a kind 'that don't just arise as you sit round the camp fire'. What was needed, he insisted, was 'clear thinking'.[68] Like Wyneken, he viewed the Wandervogel as lacking a properly intellectual stance. It made things too easy for itself; it might make people happy, but it did not make them think.

For Wyneken, Wandervogel romanticism was an 'escape from the present'. This, it seemed to him, was alright as criticism of the excesses of materialism and technology, but that was only part of the problem. 'The positive element is necessary', he said of the Wandervogel, 'and this is missing.'[69] The Wandervogel, that is to say, lacked 'intellectual rigour' and was suspicious 'of every higher aspect of culture which came from complex factors calling for hard work to understand them'.[70] It had created a youth culture of a sort, but showed 'clear signs of intellectual undernourishment'. It had 'rested content with cheap, easily accessible values and had not developed in people the attitude and strength needed for intellectual effort'. It had not awakened a 'hunger for the highest things' or any sense of 'responsibility to the mind (*Geist*)'.[71] Connected with this was his commendation of *Der Anfang*, a journal closely associated with the Freideutsche Jugend, independently controlled by young people themselves, and pursuing the ideal of a 'youth culture' in Wyneken's sense of the term. He expressed approval of the editor's remark about the need for 'intellectual loosening up', so that 'the muscles of our brain do not wither' and 'we can exercise our moral lungs'.[72] We recall the problems that arose in the Wandervogel about Hammer's book on Nietzsche — the editor of *Der Anfang* reviewed it enthusiastically.

The tension between Freideutsche Jugend and Wandervogel reflected divergences of several kinds. A critical factor was the gap dividing Wyneken from the social and political values paramount in the Wandervogel. An article in one nationalistic journal in 1913 drew a clear distinction between Wandervogel and Freideutsche Jugend on this very basis.[73] The Wandervogel, it said, was 'of pure German origin', independent of 'foreign models'. This was why it wanted to demonstrate to the young the beauties of the German countryside, to introduce them to the various ethnic groups (*Stämme*) and to German customs and folklore. It sang 'real German songs' and encouraged the 'toughening up' of German youth. In short, it was 'an important *völkisch* movement'. Contrast all this, the article said, with Wyneken's 'confused cosmopolitanism'.

Cosmopolitanism was one of the charges that nationalists laid against Nietzsche too, and how vehement was their dislike of him we shall see in the next chapter. The fact that the Wandervogel tended to be at best indifferent to Nietzsche, and Wyneken, from the point of view of the Freideutsche Jugend, to be so receptive to his ideas is thus, we may conclude, an apt commentary on these two main aspects of the Youth Movement in Wilhelmine Germany.

Notes to Chapter VIII

[1] *Werke*, I, p. 281.
[2] *Ibid.*, p. 276.
[3] Berlin, 1900.
[4] p. 326.
[5] Jena and Leipzig, 1905, pp. 274 ff.
[6] Jena, 1908.
[7] pp. 4, 10.
[8] Cf. for example, his article 'Friedrich Nietzsche', in *Die Christliche Welt* (1900),

pp. 1045 ff. Cf. Also Gerhard Kratzsch, *Kunstwart und Dürerbund: ein Beitrag zur Geschichte der Gebildeten im Zeitalter des Imperialismus* (Göttingen, 1969), where (p. 92) Bonus is referred to as a 'pupil of Lagarde, who reckoned that Nietzsche had had no great influence on him'. There is however evidence that Nietzsche's influence may have been greater than this view suggests. True, he often distanced himself somewhat from Nietzsche, but he must have been much in his mind, especially in the light of his obsession with Lebensphilosophie. This is apparent in all his works mentioned and also in his *Religiöse Spannungen: Prolegomena zu einem neuen Mythos* (Jena, 1912), pp. 173–5.

⁹ Letter to Bonus of 18 August 1900, recommending Schwann's novel, which Diederichs was shortly to publish, and which he thought would interest Bonus because of his enthusiasm for *das volle, starke Leben*. The letter is quoted in full in Lulu von Strauss and Torney (ed.), *Eugen Diederichs: Leben und Werk* (Jena, 1936), p. 54.

¹⁰ Jena, 1911.

¹¹ Cf. Diederichs, 'Lebenslauf'. Cf. Ch. VII, note 50.

¹² Friedrich Paulsen, reviewing *Vom Kulturwert der deutschen Schule*, quoted in *Hochland* (1904–5), p. 627.

¹³ In his *Nietzsche als Erzieher* (Leipzig, 1914), p. 9, for example, Walter Hammer imagines himself at one point addressing a Wandervogel who 'devoured' *Thus spake Zarathustra*.

¹⁴ *Ibid.*, pp. 26, 27.

¹⁵ Else Frobenius, *Mit uns zieht die neue Zeit: eine Geschichte der Jugendbewegung*, n. d. [1927], p. 35.

¹⁶ *Grundschriften der Jugendbewegung* (Düsseldorf and Cologne, 1963).

¹⁷ Cf. Hans Blüher, *Werke und Tage* (Munich, 1932), p. 16.

¹⁸ Cf. Rudolf Paulsen, 'Karl Fischer zum Gedenken' (1941), of which there is a typescript copy in the Archiv der deutschen Jugendbewegung at Burg Ludwigstein, to which I am greatly indebted for permission to use material from that source, liberally drawn upon in this chapter.

¹⁹ Cf. Kund Bryk, 'Erinnerung an Karl Fischer'. Copy at Burg Ludwigstein.

²⁰ Cf. *Der Neue Bund*, H. 10. Copy at Burg Ludwigstein.

²¹ Cf. Gerhard Ziemer and Hans Wolf, *Wandervogel und Freideutsche Jugend* (Bad Godesberg, 1961), p. 122.

²² It is important not to forget that the enormous popularity of Langbehn was reflected in the vast sales of his book, which a year after publication went into its thirty-seventh edition.

²³ Peter G. J. Putzer, *Die Entstehung des politischen Antisemitismus in Deutschland und Österreich 1867 bis 1910* (Gütersloh, 1966), p. 243.

²⁴ Bryk, *op. cit.*

²⁵ Cf. *Der Neue Bund*, H. 22. Copy at Burg Ludwigstein.

²⁶ Paulsen, *op. cit.*

²⁷ For comments about how Gurlitt fitted in to the Steglitz atmosphere cf. Hans Blüher, *Wandervogel: Geschichte einer Jugendbewegung*, Part I, 4th edition (Charlottenburg, 1919), pp. 34–5.

²⁸ Berlin, 1902.

²⁹ *Die Aktion* (1911), col. 266.

³⁰ 'Das Problem der nationalen Erziehung', in *Deutsche Monatsschrift für das gesamte Leben der Gegenwart* (1904), pp. 678 ff.

[31] 'Schulzeit: aus unveröffentlichten Aufzeichnungen von Karl Fischer'. Copy at Burg Ludwigstein.

[32] Cf. Hans Breuer, 'Karl Fischer: Ein Erinnerungsblatt'. Copy at Burg Ludwigstein.

[33] pp. 133–5.

[34] Oskar Stoll, 'Der Mensch als Wesenheit', in *Der Mensch*, 11 Jg., No. 10 (1904). For *Lebensreform* in the wider perspective cf. Janos Frecat, J. F. Geist, Dietrich Kerbs, *Fidus 1868–1948* (Munich, 1972).

[35] *Friedrich Nietzsche: der Lebensreformer und seine Zukunftskultur*, 2nd edition (Leipzig, 1910).

[36] *Ibid.*, p. v.

[37] For Nietzsche's experimentation with vegetarianism cf., for example, Ronald Hayman, *Nietzsche: a Critical Life* (London, 1980).

[38] pp. 46 ff.

[39] p. 46.

[40] p. 9.

[41] Letter to Walter Christaller of 17 March 1914. Copy at Burg Ludwigstein. Cf. *Nietzsche als Erzieher*, p. 5.

[42] Letter of 23 February 1914 from Hans Paasche. Copy at Burg Ludwigstein.

[43] *Führerzeitung* (1914), H. 3, p. 66.

[44] Copy at Burg Ludwigstein.

[45] Copy at Burg Ludwigstein.

[46] 'Nietzsche im Krieg', in *Die Weissen Blätter* (1919), pp. 277 ff.

[47] *Hammer*, No. 339 (1916), p. 411.

[48] 'Nochmals Weltanschauungsfragen an der Front', No. 23 (8 June 1918).

[49] Letter from Margaret Wurche to Hans Wolf of 26 April 1968. For her rather fuller account cf. the New York *Wandervogelrundbrief*, 4 (1964). Copies of both at Burg Ludwigstein.

[50] Quoted in Martin Flex's postscript to the Munich 1922 edition.

[51] Cf. Heinrich Kupffer, *Gustav Wyneken 1875–1964* (Stuttgart, 1970).

[52] *Young Germany: a History of the German Youth Movement* (London, 1962), pp. 8–9.

[53] 'Entwicklungsphasen der Freideutschen Jugend', in *Die Politik des Geistes* (Düsseldorf and Cologne, 1920), p. 119. First published in *Die Tat* (July 1918).

[54] Quoted in Martin Rockenbach (ed.), *Jugendbewegung und Dichtung* (Leipzig and Cologne, n. d.) [1924], p. 106.

[55] *In Memoriam Eugen Diederichs* (Jena, 1930).

[56] Georg Schmidt, 'Eugen Diederichs und die Jugendbewegung', in *Der Jungdeutsche* (28 October 1930).

[57] Cf. the circular, signed by Diederichs and dated 17 July 1913, inviting contributions to the Festschrift that he proposed to publish in honour of the forthcoming meeting on the Hohe Meissner. Copy at Burg Ludwigstein.

[58] *Die Politik des Geistes*, pp. 119–20.

[59] Cf. Lulu von Strauss und Torney (ed.), *op. cit.*, pp. 103–4.

[60] Bruno Lemke's speech, quoted in A. Messer, *Die freideutsche Jugendbewegung*, 5th edition (Langensalza, 1924), p. 16.

[61] Quoted in *ibid.*, p. 13.

[62] *Werke*, I, pp. 288 ff.

[63] *Ibid.*, p. 318.

[64] Cf. Hermann Buddensieg, 'Meissnerformel, Jugendkultur und neuer Aufbruch', in Werner Kindt (ed.), *op. cit.*, p. 14.

[65] Cf. Rudolf Pannwitz, 'Der Führer der deutschen Jugend'. Copy at Burg Ludwigstein.

[66] Wyneken, *Der Kampf für die Jugend*, enlarged edition (Jena, 1920), pp. 100–1.

[67] Armin Mohler, *Die konservative Revolution in Deutschland 1918–1932* (Stuttgart, 1950), p. 42.

[68] Letter dated 3 August 1916, to Arno Steglitz. Copy at Burg Ludwigstein.

[69] *Der Kampf für die Jugend*, p. 134.

[70] *Ibid.*, p. 100.

[71] *Ibid.*, p. 122.

[72] *Der Anfang* (December 1913), pp. 252–3.

[73] Siegfried Klewitz, '"Freideutsche Jugend"', in *Akademische Blätter* ('Zeitschrift des Kyffhäuser-Verbandes des Vereins Deutscher Studenten') (3 Decemeber 1913).

IX

The Alldeutsche Verband, Social Darwinism, and Nietzsche

In 1890 Germany signed a treaty with England whereby it surrendered Zanzibar in return for Heligoland. This affronted nationalist opinion in Germany, which saw the deal as the swapping of cherished colonial rights for what then seemed to be a useless bit of rock in the North Sea. The Alldeutsche Verband was founded the following year as a protest against this arrangement and as a way of advancing the nationalist cause. Its first president was Ernst Hasse. He was succeeded in 1908 by Heinrich Class, who remained the dominant figure till the Alldeutsche Verband ceased to exist in 1939. Its aim was a greater Germany stretching from Berlin to Baghdad, and it played a major part in influencing public opinion in an imperialist direction. Comparable organisations included the Deutsche Kolonialgesellschaft, the Flottenverein, the Allgemeine Deutsche Schulverein zur Erhaltung des Deutschtums im Ausland, the Ostmarkenverein and the Deutsche Sprachverein. The Alldeutsche Verband influenced them all by having members on their executive committees.

Its ideology included a strong element of Social Darwinism. Class, for example, greatly admired Willibald Hentschell, a notable Social Darwinist of the time, originator of the idea of a German utopia to which he gave the name Mittgart, and which he envisaged as a way towards the renewal of the German race. He wrote extensively on this subject, always stressing the importance of racial hygiene. What worried him was the thought of a culturally debased Germany surrounded by hostile powers, menaced by 'Jewish-democratic and jesuitical revolts', and poisoned by the influence of the cities.[1] He appealed to all those of his contemporaries who were 'seized with a sense of nausea through drinking the now so insipid waters of life', to get together and build the 'great ship' that would withstand the storms and be a safe bearer of 'life'.[2] The future would depend on 'breeding' and 'selection', and the 'weeding out of the inferior'. It was necessary, he said, to 'encourage those chosen by nature to continue the species' and to annihilate the unsuitable or at least 'see to it that they do not participate in the process of breeding'.[3]

The reference in the title of the book in question to 'higher development', the idea of a better type of man, the theme of 'life', the concept of the weak going under and the strong predominating, might well seem to imply the influence of Nietzsche, and Hentschell did say that over the entrance to Mittgart one could 'inscribe those words ... with which Nietzsche linked the mystery of racial breeding, which he foresaw in his mind's eye, with the name of Dionysus, "The noblest clay, the most precious marble, is here moulded and chiselled, namely man"'.[4] In a different connection, however, he had spoken damningly of Nietzsche and repudiated him, a fact which, as we shall see, helped Hentschell's standing with the Alldeutsche Verband.

The question of Nietzsche arises in the case of another well known Social Darwinist, Wilhelm Schallmeyer. His *Über die drohende körperliche Entartung der Kulturmenschheit* ('On the threatening physical decay of cultured mankind') appeared in 1891, but it was his *Vererbung und Auslese im Lebenslauf der Völker* ('Inheritance and selection in the life of nations') that made his name. With this book, published anonymously in the first instance, he won the prize in a competition initiated by Alfred Friedrich Krupp. Here, in passing, Schallmeyer has a few brief words in Nietzsche's favour, but only in parenthesis, and merely to claim that with his concept of the Superman he had provided the idea on which the theory of inherited characteristics and selection rested. In any case, at the climax of the book it is not Nietzsche, but Kant whom he quotes, and he likes to stress what he regards as errors and misconceptions on Nietzsche's part. With his disdain for social development, he said, he concentrated too much on the higher development of the individual, too little on society.[5]

This suggests a comparison with the most important of the German Social Darwinists at this time, Alexander Tille, author of *Volksdienst* and *Darwin und Nietzsche*. A member of the Alldeutsche Verband from 1898 and of its executive committee, Tille spent the years from 1900 to 1910 teaching German at Glasgow University. He gave up his job when the students rose up against him, accusing him of pro-Boer sympathies. Then he returned to Germany and in 1903 took an executive post with the employers' organisation in Saarbrücken. It was then that he established close relations with Freiherr von Stumm-Hallberg whose speeches he edited posthumously at the request of his family.

For Tille, a Social Darwinist of the most extreme kind, the appearance of *The Origin of Species* was so epoch-making he said, as to divide the nineteenth century into two separate halves. But of the German Social Darwinists proper in this period, none went so far in using Nietzsche in support of his philosophy. When Tille went to Glasgow, he was welcomed, according to one report, as representing 'the very last word in modes and moods fashionable with youngest Germany'. He was thought of as a 'furious Nietzschean', and he lectured on him as the 'herald of modern Germany' to the Glasgow Goethe

Society.[6] His view of Nietzsche however was of a rather brash and brutal kind. Thus Helene Stöcker, a more sensitive Nietzschean than Tille, records how deeply, in her many discussions with him, their views of Nietzsche differed. What was dear to her in Nietzsche, she said, was rejected by him, and vice versa.[7]

Moreover, despite the importance of Nietzsche for him, he was careful also to distance himself from him. He criticised him for thinking too little about racial struggle between competing elements within society, and he disliked Nietzsche's preoccupation with a dominating 'aristocratic' caste. In his book about Tille, his brother stressed that while he admired Nietzsche in some ways he was 'no mere imitator of Nietzsche, as he has often been represented by his enemies'.[8] Tille knew Nietzsche's work well, edited an English edition and translated parts of it himself, but the last thing he wanted was to be a Nietzschean. He felt, according to his brother, far above Nietzsche's one-sided attitudes.

Thus, in all three cases, with Hentschell, Schallmeyer and Tille alike, it was Nietzsche's faults that finally counted. This was even more so in the case of Otto Ammon, an influential member of the Alldeutsche Verband and a man who often lectured on its behalf. His main work *Die Gesellschafts-ordnung und ihre natürlichen Grundlagen* ('The social order and its natural foundations')[9] made a deep impression on the most prominent Alldeutsche .of all, Heinrich Class, and so is all the more important in the present context.

Central to Ammon's argument is the idea of the middle class as the vital element in the leadership of the state. But the different classes were not to be separated from each other by insurmountable barriers. This was from the point of view of the middle class and not because of any altruistic concern for the lower orders. Their social function was to instil fresh blood into the middle class and thus help to keep it fit and vigorous. The peasantry was particularly important to him from this point of view. The surplus rural population, Ammon pointed out, drifts into the towns. There, its better elements are sorted out in a process of natural selection and, duly absorbed, contribute to the general benefit. It was therefore important to support the peasantry in its struggle for existence.

Ammon is thus recognisably a spokesman of the middle class, the only class he thought, capable of a proper and national policy. With advancing industrialisation, it wants a more effective role. It is conscious, however, of the weakness of its position, its lack of experience and knowledge of how society works, and conscious too of its limited political rights. To be able to achieve what it wants, the middle class must do all it can to increase its influence in the running of society. It will then be better able to play the part to which it is 'called' in the context of the 'natural' social order.

Nietzsche comes in for heavy criticism because Ammon was concerned that the middle class needed all the strength it could muster in order to fulfil its social and political mission. Nothing was to be allowed to inhibit the vitalisation of the middle class from below. It seemed to him that Nietzsche however made this more difficult by relegating the masses for ever to the bottom. Everyone should have the chance to rise, if fitted to do so, in the body corporate of society. One must not block the way as he thought Nietzsche did. Natural selection must be free to take its course. It is not, he stated, as if the world were only there for those outstanding in mind or possessions, with the masses 'only fitted to serve as their footstool'. Therefore, he had to reject a philosophy in which only the exceptional count and the masses are seen as a 'herd created to be their servants'. The same principle applied to the middle class in the interests of which Ammon disapproved of a narrow and exclusive ruling caste. With that in mind, he said that gifted people must not remain in a subordinate capacity, doing things unworthy of them. Natural selection must be the arbiter – but not, he was careful to stress, so as to shift the political balance towards the lower sections of society, who he insisted, lacked the necessary insight to reach the right decisions.

Die Gesellschaftsordnung und ihre natürlichen Grundlagen was thus clearly directed at the interests of the middle-class public. Hence, its sub-title describes it as an 'outline of a social anthropology for the use of all educated people who think about social questions'. The policies which he thought necessary could only come from that class, in which, incidentally, he did not fail to stress the importance of entrepreneurs. But if the middle class was to come into its own – by the process of natural selection, of course – not only had the lower classes, as a source of its invigoration, not to be sealed off, but things had to be loosened up at the top. The middle class must be free to move up. If the bottom area of society was not to be closed off, neither, in the interest of the middle layer, was the upper part; hence Ammon's scorn for a too self-conscious aristocracy. Those for whom only the nobility matters, he said, were not worth talking about. Here too Nietzsche was a stumbling-block. He was too harsh for Ammon's taste as far as the lower end of society was concerned, and he made it too easy for those at the top – that, it seemed to Ammon, was the consequence of his doctrine of 'higher man' and Superman. Also, he thought, one effect of so singling out those at the top would be to distract them from the practical tasks of society. From his point of view, industry, trade and commerce were a paramount concern, and he did not want an upper class, as he put it, of idlers and decadents.

If then, Nietzsche was not exactly a popular figure with the Social

Darwinists, he was still less so in the Alldeutsche Verband. Dislike of Nietzsche was there matched by praise for Lagarde. Heinrich Class was a great admirer of Lagarde, so too was Hentschell, and likewise the publisher most particularly associated with the Alldeutsche Verband, J. F. Lehmann.

Lehmann came to the Alldeutsche Verband through connections with the nationalist movement and devoted a great deal of time and energy to its service, as he did later to the Nazi cause. A main feature of his programme was works directly related to the requirements of the Alldeutsche Verband, including its handbook. He read Lagarde's *Deutsche Schriften* during a cure at Davos before the war, with wonder and admiration, and pondered the possibility of taking him over as an author on his own list. Lagarde, he reflected, had been dead some twenty years, 'but his ideas are gradually becoming part of life'.[10] He found it 'really a pleasure to come under the influence of the thoughts of this mighty man'.[11]

Another publisher attracted to Lagarde was Eugen Diederichs — not to be confused with August Diederichs, who had an honoured place in the history of the Alldeutsche Verband as one of its keenest protagonists, and the person who is said to have suggested the epithet in its title. It would have been Eugen Diederichs himself who wrote the publicity leaflet about Lagarde ('Der nationale Gedanke jenseits der nationalen Phrase'), issued by his firm in 1913 when the centenary of the battle of Leipzig was serving as an occasion for patriotic celebrations. It stressed the need to strengthen the 'inner forces of our people'. There is no better guide, it said, than Lagarde now that 'what matters most is to give the national idea ... an organic relationship to the inner life and to man's creative powers'. Only now, it declared, are we able to appreciate Lagarde's importance as a 'great man', the 'equal of Bismarck'. Diederichs published a Lagarde anthology (*Deutscher Glaube, Deutsches Vaterland, Deutsche Bildung*) in 1913 and the following year wrote to Lagarde's widow to tell her that the task of putting into effect Lagarde's ideas increasingly occupied his attention. This edition, the only one he ever published, remained in constant demand.[12]

Lehmann was a nationalist of the simplest and, one is tempted to say, of the most revolting kind. He admired Lagarde to the exclusion of Nietzsche, in whom he seems to have had no interest whatever. It was very different with Eugen Diederichs. There was a humanist as well as a nationalist perspective in his liking for Lagarde, a concern for man's 'inner life' and 'creative powers' and his relationship to Nietzsche was protracted, decisive and profound.

Nietzsche's concept of *Persönlichkeit*, he said, had provided the starting-point for his career as publisher.[13] He remained a devoted Nietzschean, though there is at least the suggestion that until he followed Nietzsche's footsteps in a pilgrimage to Sils Maria in 1906 – acquiring there incidentally, as a sort of holy relic, the green beige covering of Nietzsche's desk – like so many people, he had known Nietzsche mainly through *Thus spake Zarathustra*. This at any rate seems to be the sense of his note that in Sils Maria 'I read widely in Nietzsche and was surprised to discover how much that I found difficult to understand in Zarathustra was a quite natural form of expression'.[14] In his efforts 'to help prepare the way for a new culture',[15] a task he pursued with deep devotion and unremitting zeal, his thoughts turned constantly to Nietzsche. He set out to issue all the books in which Nietzsche himself had taken a special interest – 'books which Nietzsche loved' was the title of one of his brochures – and the books he published on him included such notable works as Bernoulli's *Franz Overbeck und Friedrich Nietzsche* and Karl Joel's *Nietzsche und die Romantik*. In these days of our greatest spiritual decline, he wrote in 1904 about the aims of his publishing house, 'the conscience of our time is embodied in Friedrich Nietzsche'.

It is easy to make too much of Diederich's *völkisch* inclinations and to poke fun at the sun-worshipping and other eccentricities in which his Sera Circle indulged.[16] There are more important things to be said about him. If Lehmann was no more than a bigoted and philistine ideologist, Diederichs was a real and, in his way, imposing intellectual, with an uncommonly sensitive awareness of cultural complexities. The indifference of the one to Nietzsche and the preoccupation of the other with him is an outward and visible sign of the gap that separated the two publishers.

Diederichs stood consciously and boldly for the best in the German classical cultural heritage. He wanted to link up with the tradition of Wilhelm von Humboldt and saw this as a basis on which to help people 'towards a spiritual existence regardless of birth and rank'.[17] The aim for him, he said, was 'universality', as Goethe and Humboldt understood it. In Diederichs' case *völkisch* leanings were directed to humane advantage and outwards to peoples other than the Germans, with a *Volkstum* of their own no less worthy of affection and cultivation. He is a striking and rather unusual case of a man drawn to a *völkisch* philosophy who, partly for this very reason, was internationally minded.

Völkisch thought had a deep regard for the idea of society as organically knit together, and a corresponding distaste for artificial barriers within society. This attitude could easily, and often did, lead to very reactionary conclusions. In the case of Diederichs, however, it encouraged an enlightened sense of social justice, with emphasis on the need – and not for the romantically regressive reasons normally characteristic of the *völkisch* movement in this respect — to overcome divisive factors within society. It is monstrous, Diederichs said in his leaflet about Lagarde, when a 'narrow, leading upper stratum, without links below, wants to create a national life'. He followed with interest, for example, the activities of the English Fabians, published the Webbs' book in translation, and was attracted to the reforming possibilities of the English garden-city movement. He was talking in essentially *völkisch* terms when he spoke of the 'forces fermenting in the *Volk*', but, when he went on to say that this called for a 'sharpened awareness of what we all have in common',[18] the emphasis shifted to the humane implications of this idea. 'Inner renewal through humane values' was a phrase used in his statement about Lagarde, in declared opposition to a policy resting on the force of arms.

Diederichs' adherence to the concept of *Persönlichkeit* affected not only his concept of the individual, but, by extension, his attitude to the *Volk*, and from both points of view it helped to shape his characteristically humane brand of *völkisch* thinking. As regards the one, he stressed the importance of respect for the 'inner characteristics (*Anlagen*)'[19] of all people. As to the other, his emphasis on the selfhood of the *Volk* — on its *Persönlichkeit* — was to the exclusion of the expansionist ideas so conspicuous in the Alldeutsche Verband and of the repressive social and political philosophy of that organisation.

His quarrel with Max Maurenbrecher was symptomatic. When, during the war, Maurenbrecher, whose *Das Leid* he had published, expounded his by this time crudely nationalistic philosophy, Diederichs wrote to tell him how strongly he dissented. He said that while in present circumstances he agreed with him about the need to awaken feeling for the state, the 'forming of a new attitude to the state must, as far as I am concerned, be an individual matter'. Unity was important, but it had to be as an 'organic continuation' of the individual's role. Youth was now going to its death not for the defence of the state as such, but in defence of its spiritual possessions. All the more relevant therefore was the demand of the German classical writers for the unfolding of the inner life. He would for this reason have nothing to do with Maurenbrecher's 'enthusiasm for a Prussian-type view of the state' requiring obedience to imposed authority. A proper political attitude, he told Maurenbrecher, presupposes first and foremost the 'shaping of *Persönlichkeit*' and 'in the freest way possible'.[20] When the war was over Diederichs was quick to realise that, as a 'leading Deutschnationaler and a friend of the Alldeutsche', Maurenbrecher wanted to sever all connections with him.[21]

By this time Diederichs had come in for severe criticism on the part of nationalist extremists, and it was against this background that in 1917 he published a plain-speaking riposte entitled 'Die Alldeutsche Gefahr' ('The pan-German menace').[22] The Alldeutsche, he said, attack every opinion other than their own. They believe in the perfection of all things German, and view the Germans as a people called by God to rule the world. They go in for chauvinistic rhetoric, preach that Germany should become an active master-race, and 'throw their weight around'. Their ideal image of the 'determined, racially conscious German' was remarkably similar to that of the swaggering fraternity student, whose aim was to 'barge his way forward and dominate others'. The fact the Germans are so cocksure about themselves is enough to show, he said, that they cannot be the superior kind of people that the Alldeutsche make them out to be, and this lack of self-criticism 'makes the Alldeutsche menace a matter of concern for every friend of our country'. With the Alldeutsche Diederichs compares what he calls the 'cultural—political German' who, rather than seeing Germans as a people with a mission to establish order in the world, has that 'feeling about life which demands the self-unfolding of the individual up to and including the self-unfolding of the individual *Volk*', and then 'sets the unfolding of humanity as its goal'. The individual *Volksstaat* enters the 'circulation of the culture of humanity without external force', and so what *Deutschtum* should mean is granting 'to each *Volk*, as to each individual, the right to unfold its own characteristics'.[23]

The theme of the importance of selfhood, applied both to the individual and the *Volk*, links up with Diederichs' double debt to the eighteenth century and to Nietzsche. How both combine in his thinking is well illustrated in his reply in the same year to an article in which the Alldeutsche had attacked him.[24] Why, he asked, is the spirit of that article so un-German? Partly because the German spirit loves 'truthfulness' (*Wahrhaftigkeit* is a word common in Nietzsche's vocabulary). It is also partly because the German spirit despises — as, he well knew, Nietzsche said it should be despised — the 'clamour of the streets'. To be German, Diederichs says, means above all 'to seek the law of one's own spiritual and cultural development', and at the same time to love 'every creature who with ourselves shares the burden of life'. Nietzsche would have branded these self-righteous Germans 'people who conjure and juggle with the German conscience', and, as to our classical writers, would they ever, he asked, 'for one single moment have sat down at the same table with their leaders?'.

However, it was not necessarily a sign of Nietzsche's influence when a writer made much of the idea of *Persönlichkeit*, though, as we have seen, his effect was often to encourage people to do so. Also, the uses to which it was put were not always by any means particularly civilised and humane. In Ernst Krieck's *Persönlichkeit und Kultur* (1910), for example, the concept acquires disturbing activistic, not to say imperialistic features, which make it not surprising that the author ended up as a leading Nazi educationalist. Nietzsche, however, plays no part in it, for Krieck's model is Lagarde.

The same applies in the comparable case of Friedrich Lange, a man well known and much respected in and around the Alldeutsche Verband. Born in 1852, he was for some years a journalist on a regional newspaper before in 1882 (till 1895) becoming editor of the *Tägliche Rundschau*. Then in 1896 he founded the *Deutsche Zeitung*, which he ran till 1912, when he retired.[25] By this time he was the well-known author of an influential book *Reines Deutschtum*, first published in 1891.[26] Here he speaks about the 'judgement-seat of *Persönlichkeit*', to which, as he puts it, the 'norm is now returning'.[27] At the same time as treating *Persönlichkeit* in this elevated way, he character-ises it in terms of energy and thrust, as Krieck did, and, like him he embodied in his idea of *Persönlichkeit* values recognisable as those of the age of im-perialism.

As an ultra-nationalist Lange called for the consolidation of Germans abroad, for a 'renewal of the Germanic migration of the peoples' as a 'great and planned enterprise in colonisation',[28] and for the rejection of the 'lunacy of cosmopolitanism'.[29] This helps to explain his admiration for Otto Ammon. He was a close friend of Lange, became one of his collaborators on the *Deutsche Zeitung*, and figures in *Reines Deutschtum* because of an article he had written about the significance of China in a world-historical context. Lange was impressed by the fact that Ammon saw the struggle beginning in China as the 'first serious attempt of the whole white race to bring the yellow race under the power of Aryan culture'[30] — which Ammon regarded as indispensable for economic reasons. Lange was pleased to note that he viewed China, with its coal and mineral resources and its supply of cheap labour, as able to satisfy the need of the white race to extend its economic sphere of influence. This was exactly what Lange wanted to hear, and it was not, he commented, by any means 'too bold a dream'.[31]

From Lange's point of view, however, there was obviously no joy to be got from a man like Nietzsche, who identified himself with those who 'are not nearly "German" enough ... to speak out for nationalism and racial hatred'.[32] 'Think German, feel German', Nietzsche said, 'I can do anything, but that is quite beyond me.'[33] His image of himself as the 'good European' would not be an endearing feature either, nor was the nice way he sometimes spoke about Jews. He even sneered at Treitschke, who was to become a hero of the Alldeutsche Verband: 'At the Prussian court, I fear, they regard Herr von Treitschke as a profound thinker'.[34] So we have to be careful not to jump to conclusions when we find Lange talking about *Persönlichkeit* in terms of 'fully creative people', the manifestation of 'heightened life-force'. That may sound a bit Nietzschean, but there is no actual connection. Lange was a declared enemy of Nietzsche, while high on the list of those he admired was Gobineau.

Thus, in 1900 Lange wrote an essay,[35] reprinted in later editions of *Reines Deutschtum*, in which he compared the two men, praising the one as much as he condemned the other. He even apologised for so much as coupling the name of that 'mighty monumental architect' with someone who merely 'built flimsy structures out of thin air'. His purpose in so doing was thereby to rectify the current 'inordinate admiration' of Nietzsche on the part of 'literati and neurotics'. He could not even find any good to say about the 'aristocratic' features in Nietzsche's philosphy. With Gobineau, he said, they came from the blood, but with Nietzsche merely from the imagination, so all one gets from him is the 'whiff of aristocracy', so appealing to Jewish intellectuals. If writers admire Zarathustra on his lonely heights, it is because doing so satisfies their conceit, and never has a philosopher made it easier than Nietzsche, with his gospel of the Superman, 'for artistic people and hysterical women' to 'feel the equal of the gods'. However, for the man they so applaud, Lange says, 'birth and rank, *Volk* and nation, morality and religion, are as nothing'. Nietzsche's mind was diseased, and his scorn for nationality proves it: 'the nearer one gets to the madhouse, the more certain one is to be on the right road to becoming a good European'.

Lange's dismissive view of Nietzsche was typical of the attitude current within the Alldeutsche Verband generally, and his reasons were much the same. Prominent among them was the question of the moral status of the Superman. As Otto Bonhard said in his more or less official history of the Alldeutsche Verband, it was not that it did not recognise that the best derives from the chosen few, from which follows 'the "heroic" view of life which we Alldeutsche honour and to which we owe the manly element in our thinking'; but it is dangerous if one 'falsifies the hero into the "Superman"'.[36] From an ethical point of view the Superman seemed a dubious sort of character to an organisation which prided itself so self-righteously on its role in upholding moral values. The freedom from control, *Schrankenlosigkeit*, in Nietzsche's master-morality worried Bonhard as it did Ammon. The concept of a highly-placed minority behaving as it liked was not to be tolerated, and the notion of the Superman seemed to point in that direction. Bonhard's position is very close to Ammon's and his reasons, similarly, are the interests of the middle class. It will be recalled that Ammon, with his idea of the benefits accruing to the middle class from below, criticised Nietzsche for debasing those at the bottom of the social scale too much and he wanted more than a select few to be able to rule at the top. Bonhard was of the same mind. Nietzsche, he said reprovingly, 'strained the idea of inequality'.

Bonhard insisted that 'we have absolutely nothing in common' with concepts like Nietzsche's. He was so emphatic because some people had tried to connect Nietzsche with the Alldeutsche Verband in order to discredit it by association. This was why he made so much of Nietzsche's doctrines as morally suspect and in the same connection, of the fact that the only leaders of the future which the Alldeutsche could envisage, in contrast to Nietzsche's Superman, were 'heroes of moral greatness'. It was also why he was so keen to assure his readers that there was no evidence 'that any of the leading Alldeutsche had a close relationship to Nietzsche's thought'.[37]

All other considerations apart, Nietzsche's frequently expressed pro-Jewish sympathies were in themselves enough to make him *persona non grata* in nationalist circles generally. It was as a friend of the Jews that Nietzsche was presented, for example, by Theodor Fritsch, editor of the main anit-Jewish paper, the *Antisemitische Correspondenz*, and a vociferously anti-Nietzsche (and pro-Lagarde) propagandist in the nationalist paper *Hammer*. In 1887, under the pseudonym Thomas Frey, he had published an article in the *Antisemitische Correspondenz*[38] expressing indignation about *Beyond Good and Evil* as a 'glorification of the Jews', a 'condemnation of anti-semitism', and the specious chatter of a 'non-scholar tarred with the Jewish brush (*eines angejudelten Stuben-Verlehrten*)'. This greatly impressed Willibald Hentschell, and we soon find him saying, likewise in the *Antisemitische Correspondenz*, that while he had once thought well of Nietzsche, he now realised, in the light of Fritsch's article, the extent of his 'love of the Jews' and regarded him as the 'victim of a dying age' – despite his suggestion meanwhile that Nietzsche might provide a motto for Mittgart, his idea of a German utopia mentioned at the beginning of this chapter.[39] But in any case, this has to be set against his denigrating comment on a speaker at the Conference of German Scientists and Doctors in 1909 who had talked about 'breeding'. Hentschell objected that this was 'in the sense of breeding the "Superman"', and 'our cause is poorly served by idiocies of that kind'.[40] So we can appreciate Bonhard's comment on Hentschell as one who, though an outsider as far as the Alldeutsche Verband was concerned, propounded ideas commendably close to its own. Fritsch for his part persisted with his attacks on Nietzsche, as a man whose thinking was 'unmanly, womanish, coquettish', one of those people who 'bring disease into our age'[41] – and that would have been the generally accepted view within the Alldeutsche Verband.

Notes to Chapter IX

[1] *Vom aufsteigenden Leben* ('Ziele der Rassen-Hygiene') (Leipzig and Hamburg, 2nd edition, n. d.), p. 43.

[2] *Ibid.*, p. 118.

[3] *Ibid.*, p. 126.

[4] *Ibid.*, p. 123.

[5] Cf. Hedwig Conrad-Martius, *Utopien der Menschenzüchtung* (Munich, 1955), pp. 74 ff.

[6] Quoted in Krummel, *op. cit.*, pp. 134–5 n.

[7] Cf. Helene Stöcker's 'Lebensabriss', in which connection cf. Chapter VII, note 37.

[8] Armin Tille, *Ein Kämpferleben: Alexander Tille 1866–1912* (Gotha, 1916), p. 37.

[9] 3rd revised edition (Jena, 1900).

[10] Letter of 16 August 1908, quoted in Melanie Lehmann (ed.), *Verleger J. F. Lehmann: Ein Leben im Kampf für Deutschland* (Munich, 1936), p. 111.

[11] Letter of 30 December 1918, quoted in *ibid.*, pp. 159–160.

[12] For some comments by Diederichs himself on his relation to Lagarde, cf. his autobiographical contribution to the Diederichs Festschrift *Eugen Diederichs: sein Leben und sein Werk* (Leipzig, 1927), p. 40.

[13] Cf. p. 106, where the remark is quoted from Lulu von Strauss und Torney's book. It occurs also in the 'Lebenslauf', for which cf. Chapter VII, note 50.

[14] 'Lebenslauf', where however the pagination makes reference very difficult.

[15] Letter to Otto Jimmisch of 23 September 1910, in *Eugen Diederichs: Selbstzeugnisse und Briefe von Zeitgenossen* (Düsseldorf and Cologne, 1967), p. 189.

[16] As, I think, G. L. Mosse is inclined to do in *The Crisis of German Ideology* (London, 1966), pp. 53 ff.

[17] *Eugen Diederichs: Selbstzeugnisse und Briefe von Zeitgenossen*, p. 42.

[18] *Ibid.*, p. 42.

[19] *Ibid.*, p. 42.

[20] Lulu von Strauss und Torney (ed.), *op. cit.*, pp. 280–1.

[21] *Ibid.*, p. 369.

[22] *Die Tat* (September 1917), pp. 518 ff.

[23] Diederichs had stated the same principle in one of his annual handouts, 'Die deutsche Kulturbewegung im Jahre 1913', where he stressed the 'complementary characteristics of other nations' as a warning to steer clear of chauvinistic rhetoric – this helps to put into perspective his remark in the same context about German *Volkstum* requiring 'conscious racial feeling'.

[24] 'Zu einem alldeutschen Angriff', in *Die Politik des Geistes*.

[25] Cf. Arnold Leinemann, *Friedrich Lange und die Deutsche Zeitung* (Diss., Berlin, 1928).

[26] 3rd enlarged edition (Berlin, 1904).

[27] *Ibid.*, p. 72.

[28] *Ibid.*, p. 205.

[29] *Ibid.*, p. 353.

[30] *Ibid.*, p. 231.

[31] *Ibid.*, p. 233.

[32] *Werke*, II, p. 253.

[33]   *Ibid.*, p. 1102.
[34]   *Ibid.*, p. 1150.
[35]   'Gobineau und Nietzsche', in *Reines Deutschtum*, pp. 248 ff.
[36]   *Geschichte des Alldeutschen Verbandes* (Leipzig and Berlin, 1920), p. 186. For the history of the Alldeutsche Verband cf. also Alfred Kruck, *Geschichte des Alldeutschen Verbandes 1890–1939* (Wiesbaden, 1954), and Heinrich Class, *Wider den Strom* (1932).
[37]   Bonhard, p. 187.
[38]   Krummel, *op. cit.*, pp. 65–6.
[39]   Quoted in *ibid.*, p. 76.
[40]   *Vom aufsteigenden Leben*, p. 16 n.
[41]   'Nietzsche und die Jugend', in *Hammer* (1 March 1911), pp. 113 ff.

Conclusion

Regarding the situation in Germany around 1900, one distinguished German historian mentions the aggressive talk about *Lebensraum*, connects it with 'the modern *Lebensphilosophie* represented above all by Nietzsche', refers to the 'glorification of the strong-willed *Herrenmensch*', and finds Nietzsche guilty of 'pushing into the shade humanitarian and pacifistic tendencies'.[1] This chain of associations reflects the common — and all too little investigated — assumption that Nietzsche was a major factor behind the harsher features of Wilhelmine Germany.

It is easy, of course, to see how this idea could arise. On the one hand, a thinker with 'will to power' (as an inescapable fact of life) at the heart of his philosophy, on the other, a state notoriously fond of exercising it even at the cost of war — the association could well seem irresistible.

Our study, however, does not support it. In a nutshell, there were no more committed and influential exponents of the expansionist doctrine of *Lebensraum* than the Alldeutsche and their friends, and we have seen what *they* thought of Nietzsche. As to the idea of the Superman, the apogee of the *Herrenmensch*, it was they who least wanted to have anything to do with it. Of course, individual cases can always be found which deviate from the general pattern. Maximilian Harden, for example,[2] editor of *Die Zukunft*, was an intellectual who became fascinated by politics as a world dominated by the will to power in action. This led him to admire Nietzsche as its great theorist and Bismarck, the 'most mighty individualist', as its supreme practitioner.[3]

However, it is with organised forums of opinion, with social and political aims, that we are concerned as the touchstone, practically speaking, of Nietzsche's impact. We have therefore identified and examined those sectors of German politics and society where Nietzsche was important one way or another, positively or negatively. What the evidence shows on this basis is that in this period Nietzsche was most likely to be welcomed as a friend where there was an oppositional urge resisting pressure to obey and conform. Where he was prone to be viewed with least respect was among the people closest to the cruder extremes of nationalism and committed to the social, economic and political priorities associated with it.

Of course, there were those who were drawn at one stage to Nietzsche for broadly speaking, emancipatory reasons and moved on to a nationalistic position. Josef Bloch is one such case, Maurenbrecher another, and so is Lily Braun, bearing in mind her shift of attitude when the war came. It is easy in such instances to compare what was admired in Nietzsche initially for non-nationalistic reasons with values — will, energy, resolution, power and so forth — which find scope in war, conquest and repression. It is equally easy then to think in terms of cause and effect. There may indeed be hidden connections, but in the circumstances it is just as likely in cases such as these that they would have veered to nationalism even without Nietzsche in the background. Indeed, in the context of the situation in Germany at the time, with public opinion being pushed more and more in the direction of expansionism and chauvinism, this is less a possibility than a probability. Above all, Nietzsche's unpopularity among the exponents of attitudes and policies with nationalist associations would tempt us to see the position in that light.

If, however, it were to prove to be the case that, when the time came, Nietzsche's ideas were generally welcomed as an aid to the ideology of Germany's war-effort after 1914, things might look a little different. Our evidence, with the emphasis it puts on Nietzsche's libertarian influence, would look less secure. What then are the facts?

There were indeed, briefly, signs of his being drawn into the picture for propaganda purposes. Several items to this effect appeared in the influential *Berliner Tageblatt*. This however evoked a strong riposte from Franz Pfemfert in his journal *Die Aktion*. His reaction is the more interesting since his sympathies were all on the side of emancipation. Pacifist, anarcho-syndicalist and revolutionary, he was intolerant of anything and anyone seeming to lend support in any way to power-political and authoritarian values. All the more significant therefore is his indignation at what he called the *Deutschsprechung* of Nietzsche, that is of his being declared a good and true German, worthy ally of the nationalist cause. After all that Nietzsche had said and what had been said about him, he thought this a 'monstrous thing to happen' to someone who so obviously loathed Prussia and Germany. He found it 'quite incredible'.[4]

One of the people he referred to in connection with the *Berliner Tageblatt* was the philosopher Fritz Mauthner. Mauthner regretted that philosophy's contribution had been relatively slight: mathematics, even literature and painting were more fortunate in this respect. In his view, philosophers had only themselves to blame. They were far too inclined to talk about war as contrary to reason and of peace as the only rational prospect. At least, he went on, this was the case 'until Nietzsche came, despised pity, and praised war'.[5] It was a passing mention, but it served to make Nietzsche look highly respectable. Apart from other less notable figures represented in the same paper, Pfemfert mentioned also the economist Werner Sombart, though his main contribution to the discussion of Nietzsche and war was elsewhere, in his book *Händler und Helden* (1915). Mauthner was not an academic proper, but Sombart was — and one of the few who used Nietzsche as an aid to war propaganda.[6]

Sombart's general idea in *Händler und Helden* was of the war with England as one between 'tradesmen' and 'heroes', with the commercially-minded English governed only by the principle of the greatest happiness of the greatest number. 'We find quite horrible', he remarks, quoting *Thus spake Zarathustra*, 'the degenerating mind which says that everything exists to serve my own advantage.' The German motivation, he said, was deeper and more authentic. There had been a long line of prophets proclaiming the news 'that it is the German people that gave birth to the son of God'. Nietzsche was the latest of these prophets and the Superman the most recent in this line of descent. This therefore was 'Nietzsche's war', and also the war of Frederick the Great, Goethe, Schiller, Beethoven, Hegel and Bismarck. In this company Nietzsche was 'at one with the German spirit and thus worthy of being regarded as at home in Weimar and Potsdam'.[7]

Statements like these, however, were wildly out of keeping with the predominantly anti-Nietzsche pronouncements provoked by the war, despite occasional anthologies like Max Brahn's *Friedrich Nietzsches Meinungen über Staaten und Kriege* ('Nietzsche's views on states and wars')[8] and Hermann Itscher's *Nietzsche-Worte: Weggenossen in grosser Zeit* ('Sayings of Nietzsche: companions in a great time').[9] Also, *Der Kampf des deutschen Geistes* ('The struggle of the German spirit'), by various hands,[10] takes its motto-quotation from Nietzsche, makes introductory passing reference to Nietzsche, and — grotesquely — describes him as believing that Germans were destined to play the leading part in the new age. In the body of the book however Nietzsche is well and truly rejected. The charge against him is one with which we are now familiar from nationalist quarters, namely, his failure as far as moral values are concerned. He cannot possibly qualify as the 'philosophical commander' of Germans in their present struggle or as a 'national philosopher'.[11] When an article appeared in one paper praising Nietzsche as having helped to prepare the way for the war, this prompted a warning in the conservative religious press that his 'will to power' rested on a brutal and immoral basis and had nothing to do with the sublime spirit motivating Germany at war.[12]

He came off no better in a series of 'patriotic' lectures by the Leipzig historian Karl Lamprecht, entitled *Krieg und Kultur* ('War and culture'),[13] where again he is associated with moral degeneracy, and his immoralism is said to disqualify him from any place in arguments involving the nobility of the German people and its cause. Lamprecht found the idea of the Superman very troublesome — an 'exaggerated solution', he thought, to the problems of the future.[14]

Nietzsche's idea of the 'blond beast' was embarrassing too. The danger was felt to be that people might identify this with the blond Teuton and associate beast and German. The 'blond man' — the German, that is to say — one nationalist journal was keen to point out, is 'farthest removed from the beast'.[15] A book on Nietzsche published during the war, and obviously designed for popular consumption, stressed in its title Nietzsche as 'immoralist' and 'anti-Christ', though on balance it is surprisingly restrained, with a moderately positive conclusion.[16] All the same, the paper just referred to, concerned about the fact that German soldiers were said to be busy reading *Thus spake Zarathustra*, thought it an effective enough attack on Nietzsche to recommend it as an eminently suitable volume to send the troops as a greeting from home.[17] It is worthy of note too that when Maurenbrecher, who had earlier drawn so heavily on Nietzsche, became the complete nationalist, Nietzsche faded out of the picture, and he carefully avoids mentioning him in his war book *Neue Staatsgesinnung*,[18] though the stress there on the force of the will might have given him every excuse to do so.

Despite all this, Nietzsche came, especially abroad, to be lumped together with German nationalists and militarists as sharing responsibility for the war. One London bookseller displayed the English edition of Nietzsche's works with the notice, 'The Euro-Nietzschean war. Read the Devil in order to fight him the better'. By 1915, Thomas Mann noted from a report in the *Frankfurter Zeitung*[19] that Nietzsche was being linked in England with the nationalist historian Treitschke and with General Friedrich von Bernhardi, author of *Deutschland und der nächste Krieg* ('Germany and the next war')[20] — 'a grotesque cacophony', Mann said later, 'for the ear of all intellectual Germans ...'.[21] It was ridiculous, he added, 'that Nietzsche should be brought in to complete the symbol of German wickedness'. It was all the more so since Nietzsche despised Treitschke, and Treitschke him, and the association with Bernhardi stemmed only from an out-of-context quotation from Nietzsche, with which he prefaced his book. Apart from that, it had as good as nothing to do with Nietzsche.

The hero of *Deutschland und der nächste Krieg* is not Nietzsche but Kant,[22] and it is on him that Bernhardi — who was not unique among senior German officers in his interest in philosophy[23] — relies for support for his doctrines. For him, Kant's philosophy constitutes the second great movement in Germany after the Reformation, with *The Critique of Pure Reason* as the other half of the basis of the intellectual life of our time. Prussia inaugurated the concept of duty and moral duty is Kant's key concept.[24] It is from Kant that Bernhardi derives the notion of subordinating individual happiness to the needs of the state, and the justification of universal military service. So his book is not really about Nietzsche at all. That it came to lend support to the idea of Nietzsche as encouraging the ideology of war rested on an extraordinary misconception and goes to show what a chance quotation can do.

In any case, Nietzsche could not legitimately be enrolled in the service of any ideology. Against the 'tied spirit (*gebundene Geist*)' that demands 'belief', he was for the 'free spirit', interested only in the 'reasons why'.[25] Bring *Erkenntnis*, understanding, than which 'no honey is sweeter', to bear on all experience, he said, 'play carefully the game with the scales "on the one hand", "on the other"'.[26] Be cautious in the face of every grand word and posture – to need convictions is to falsify oneself. 'We men of today', he commented, are 'against ultimate convictions', we have a 'distaste for great moral pronouncements and gestures'.[27] Hence that 'multi-dimensional abundance', which Jaspers found so characteristic of Nietzsche's thought, as reflected in those darting, aphoristic features typical of much of his style. Contradiction was for him a necessary part of existence, the greatest step of all for the liberated spirit, unsettling the familiar and the sacrosanct. Harmony, he insisted, was mere appearance.

It is understandable therefore, and worthy of comment as we look back on the use of Nietzsche's ideas in the political and social life of Wilhelmine Germany, that, while he was sometimes keen to have disciples, at other times he was not too sure. His less obviously ingratiating features – a type of argument, for example, sometimes calculated to shock rather than to persuade – might even suggest that he was trying to put people off. It was not necessary, he said, for people to take his side and, he did not even want people to do so, preferring, as a more intelligent attitude towards him, an ironic mood of resistance. The very reference to a 'public', he said, reminded him of brothels and prostitutes. If you want supporters then what you need is nonentities, but without 'blind pupils' 'no man and his work have ever come to exercise a great influence', and 'to bring about the triumph of an idea often merely means so pairing it with studipidy that it is this that makes it victorious'.[28]

He himself thought that every great teacher can just as well, as a result of chance and circumstances, become a misfortune for mankind as a blessing. He once said that he was frightened to think how one day people would appeal to his authority, without justification who were quite unsuited to do so. It would hardly have surprised him, therefore, to discover that one day, as regards National Socialism, it would be said of his thought that it 'created a spiritual atmosphere in which certain things became possible'.[29] However, his popularity in the period of German fascism does not necessarily by any means prove that he helped to originate it, though, as Karl Löwith remarks, it was certainly no mere coincidence that he came to be so much admired by the Nazis — and by Mussolini too for that matter.

For it was one thing when, as regards ideals of selfhood around which the appeal of Nietzsche in Wilhelmine Germany tended to revolve, it was a matter of people caught in circumstances that they could sometimes be forgiven for experiencing as elements in a restrictive and oppressive system. It was another when, as with National Socialism, the enemies of libertarian ideas set about marshalling irrationalist arguments against order of a different kind, against democratic order, which, for reactionary reasons, they found tiresome and frustrating. Then, with the idea of selfhood maximised in the concept of the charismatic personality, and this in the *Führerprinzip*, what J. P. Stern nicely called Nietzsche's 'pathos of personal authenticity',[30] and other features of his philosophy — most obviously, 'will to power' — came to be instrumental in fostering the idolatry bestowed on Nietzsche by the Nazis.[31] The irony, of course, is in the fact that these people were essentially the natural successors of the nationalists and the like in Wilhelmine Germany who had most calumniated him.

Hindsight in the light of that development has been allowed to colour assumptions about Nietzsche's influence in earlier days far too much, and it is all the more important, therefore, as this book has tried to do, to get the record straight.

Notes to Conclusion

[1] Gerhard Ritter, *Staatskunst und Kriegshandwerk*, II (Munich, 1962), p. 136.
[2] Cf. Uwe Weller, *Maximilian Harden und die "Zukunft"* (Bremen, 1970), pp. 105 ff.
[3] *Apostata* (Neue Folge) (Berlin, 1892), p. 24.
[4] *Die Aktion* (26 June 1915), pp. 320 ff.
[5] *Berliner Tageblatt* (11 October 1914).
[6] Cf. Klaus Schwabe, *Wissenschaft und Kriegsmoral: die deutschen Hochschullehrer und die politischen Grundfragen des ersten Weltkrieges* (Göttingen, Zurich and Frankfurt am Main, 1969), pp. 29, 496 n.
[7] pp. 53 ff.
[8] Leipzig, 1916.

⁹ Leipzig, 1915.

¹⁰ Edited by Karl Hönn (Gotha, 1915).

¹¹ pp. 80, 78.

¹² Cf. *Der Gral* H. 1 and 2 (1917), pp. 69—70.

¹³ Leipzig, 1914.

¹⁴ p. 63.

¹⁵ Theodor Fritsch, 'Kriegsgeschichtliche Betrachtungen (2)', in *Hammer* (November 1918), pp. 561 ff.

¹⁶ Julius Reiner, *Nietzsche: der Immoralist und Antichrist* (Stuttgart, 1916).

¹⁷ *Hammer* (August 1916), p. 410.

¹⁸ Jena, 1916.

¹⁹ Cf. *Thomas Mann an Ernst Bertram: Briefe aus den Jahren 1910—1955* (Pfüllingen, 1960), p. 25.

²⁰ Berlin, 1913.

²¹ Quoted in *Thomas Mann an Ernst Bertram*, p. 210.

²² As was indeed pointed out long ago by John Dewey in his *German Philosophy and Politics*, 1915 (Revised edition, New York, 1942), pp. 74ff.

²³ An interesting case was that of Colonel Max Bauer, a staff officer in charge of heavy artillery before and during the war, a great critic of Bethmann-Hollweg, whom he accused of lacking 'creative strength' and who he thought would have benefited from reading Kant and Nietzsche (cf. *Der grosse Krieg in Feld und Heimat: Erinnerungen und Betrachtungen* (2nd edition Tübingen, 1921), pp. 142, 143). It was Kant, however, who particularly impressed him with his morality of duty. Cf. Adolf Vogt, *Oberst Max Bauer: Generalstabs-Offizier im Zwielicht 1869—1929* (Osnabrück, 1974), p. 174.

²⁴ Cf. Bernhardi's praise of Kant from much the same point of view in *Die Zukunft* (Stuttgart, 1912), p. 14.

²⁵ *Werke*, I, pp. 585—6.

²⁶ *Ibid.*, p. 623—4.

²⁷ *Werke*, II, p. 250.

²⁸ *Werke*, I, p. 528.

²⁹ Cf. Karl Löwith's introduction to his selection of Nietzsche's texts, *Zeitgemässes und Unzeitgemässes* (Frankfurt and Hamburg, 1956), p. 11.

³⁰ *Nietzsche* (London, 1978), p. 79.

³¹ For a concise discussion of the relevant aspects from this point of view, cf. Crane Brinton, *Nietzsche* (Cambridge, Mass., 1941), pp. 98 ff. Cf. also, among many other possibilities, Alfred Gut, 'Nietzsche's "Neue Barbaren"', in Hans Steffen, *Nietzsche: Werk und Wirkungen* (Gottingen, 1974).

Appendix
Nietsche, women, and the whip

Some of the German feminists, as we saw, were Nietzsche enthusiasts and used his writings to radical effect in support of their ideals. They did not bother much about the nastier things that Nietzsche sometimes said about women[1] and were not even put off by his most notorious remark of all: 'You're going to see women? Then don't forget your whip!'.[2] There was no reason why they should have done for it is not remotely about what men should do to women. What then is it about?

The words in question were first jotted down by Nietzsche in the second half of 1882, together with what appears to be a comment on them: 'In the way one shows honour, and in what one honours, one always sets oneself at a distance'.[3] Since they are easily taken as a sign of Nietzsche's contempt for women it is important to notice that on their first appearance these words are associated, as this comment shows, with respect. It needs to be stressed too, since it is Nietzsche himself who is usually thought to have said that men needed a whip in the company of women, that, when the words appear in the section 'Of women old and young' in the first part of *Thus spake Zarathustra*, where we read of Zarathustra's encounter with an old woman, it is she – a fictional character, and a female one at that – who makes the pronouncement. There is a further reference to it in 'The second dancing song' in the third part. This harks back to 'The dancing song' in the second part, likewise an integral feature of the general context.

The pre-history of the image of the whip in Nietzsche's private life is also important. In March 1882 the philosopher Paul Rée made the acquaintance of Lou Andreas-Salomé at the house of Malwida von Meysenbug in Rome, and fell in love with her. Lou, however, was not drawn to the idea of getting married and had in mind the possibility of living with two men at the same time. So he turned his mind to a possible partner in such an arrangement, and thought of Nietzsche. Nietzsche had met Lou some time before and now himself wanted to marry her. Approached on his behalf by Rée, Lou however rejected his proposal. He got the same answer when, personally this time, he proposed to Lou again, though she expressed the hope that all three would remain good friends. Nietzsche thought this a good idea, worth commemorating. So at his suggestion they all went off to a well-known photographer in Lucerne whose studio, it turned out, contained, among a number of props, a small pony-trap. Nietzsche had the idea of positioning himself with Rée between the shafts, with Lou in the driver's seat, holding a whip extemporised by Nietzsche from bits and pieces lying around. This provided the photograph that was taken. So, compared with the old woman's injunction in *Thus spake Zarathustra*, the situation is here reversed. It is, at Nietzsche's instigation, the woman who brandishes the whip, and it is the men who are the potential victims.

When, later in the same year, Nietzsche began work on *Thus spake Zarathustra*, the first part of which he had completed by February 1883, he knew full well that Lou would never be his, and it is generally agreed that the experience with Lou was a decisive factor in the genesis of that work. She was directly responsible, Overbeck said, 'for having led Nietzsche to formulate ... an alternative to religion and morality',[4] and it was in the same work that Nietzsche for the first time made a major feature explicitly of 'will to power' and of the Superman.

In the short period between Lou's refusal of Nietzsche and the point at which he embarked on writing *Thus spake Zarathustra*, Lou and Nietzsche were separately jotting down ideas which, in the light of the image of the whip as it figures there, are strangely suggestive. For Lou hatred is 'an even more intensive interest than love'; 'whom we hate is surer of our interest than whom we love', and 'love can be more than feeling for a person, it can be a fight'.[5] What a woman leans on in her weakness, Nietzsche noted, 'is not in all circumstances power that she has actually recognised, but power that she wants and has imagined', and the weaker a woman feels, 'the more power she will feel in him who "gives her support"'. 'The weakest woman', he wrote, 'will make every man into a god: and likewise she will make out of every moral and religious commandment something holy, untouchable, final, worthy to be worshipped.' So it is clear, he added, 'that, as far as the origin of religion is concerned, the weaker sex is more important than the stronger', and, given the nature of women, 'they would, if one left them alone, not only create "men" from out of their own weakness, but even "gods" – and both presumably resembling each other – as monsters of power'.[6]

Whatever we choose to make of these remarks in the critical phase before mention of the whip found its way into *Thus spake Zarathustra*, there is the hint of a relationship to Nietzsche's use of the image in that work, and this too should give us grounds for sensing that what is involved is likely to amount to nothing so simple as a recipe for maltreating women.

Normally in *Thus spake Zarathustra* the pattern is for Zarathustra to make the telling statements, but in 'Of women old and young' the crucial insight –

the remark about the whip — comes from somebody else, and it is Zarathustra who is taken by surprise. This situation arises through his meeting
an old acquaintance who notices that he seems to be hiding something
under his cloak. Zarathustra is obviously keen to conceal and cherish it,
and his friend quickly realises that he regards it as very precious. It is, Zarathustra explains, a 'tiny truth', difficult to carry around without it being
noticed, and troublesome too, 'impatient like a small child'. Usually Zarathustra is keen to proclaim what he knows, to give others the benefit of his
wisdom, but this time he is set on secrecy. How he came to possess this
'tiny truth', and why he will not talk about it, emerges from a passing conversation with a 'little old woman'. When he encountered her, he had used
the opportunity to make, as usual, a number of lofty and axiomatic pronouncements. The old woman, whom no doubt he took at first to be rather
a simple soul, listened with particular interest, so much so that she was
moved to reward him for what he had said. She did this by making him a
present of the 'tiny truth'. But she warned him that it needed careful hand-
ling. Keep its mouth shut, she told him, 'or else this tiny truth will shout
too loud'. The gift in question takes the form of a piece of advice, namely,
'you're going to see women? Then don't forget your whip!'. Zarathustra
realises at once that this amounts to something very special — he certainly
does not receive it as if it were a crude exhortation to batter women. Also,
he recognises that it is fit only for the few and the wise. No doubt he is
encouraged in this by the fact that the old woman had communicated it to
him in a whisper — inviting comparison perhaps with Goethe's words about
'telling it only to the wise, because the mob will immediately make fun of
it':

> Sagt es niemand, nur den Weisen,
> Weil die Menge gleich verhöhnet.

If there are indeed overtones here of 'Selige Sehnsucht', this may not be
entirely unintended — there will be more to say about this later.

What induced the old woman to come out with her little secret, and to
entrust it to someone she had never met before, was, we recall, the fact that
Zarathustra's remarks had appealed to her. They were a string of more or
less disconnected pronouncements, but all the same it is possible to identify
a theme. Moreover it is one that calls to mind motifs noted down earlier
by Nietzsche and Lou, involving relations between men and women from the
perspectives of 'fear', 'hatred', and 'obedience'. 'In your love', Zarathustra
had said, 'let there be bravery! You should lovingly turn on him who inspires
you with fear', 'let the man be afraid of woman when she hates', 'women

must obey'. The themes of fear, hatred and obedience on the one hand, and the image of the whip on the other have an obviously suggestive association, and one can better understand why the old woman's remark, 'you're going to see women? Then don't forget to take your whip!', so alerted Zarathustra, and why his statements so caught her attention.

Apart from the fact that it was not Nietzsche who made this remark, and not even Nietzsche–Zarathustra, it is for other reasons hardly imaginable that Nietzsche would have wanted to identify himself with its literal meaning. His relation to women in real life — respectful, tender, even coy — was not such that one can picture him wanting to flog them or wanting anyone else to do so. Nor is there, incidentally, the slightest evidence that people were in the habit of acting on Nietzsche's supposed advice. Max Nettlau was talking wildly when he spoke of young people who, led my Nietzsche into seeing themselves as *Herrenmenschen*, 'took a whip with them when they went to women'.[7] Moreover, the runic, even mystifying style of discourse in this context should be another reason for suspecting that the issue is more sophisticated than one of assault and battery.

We compared the spirit in which the old woman confided her secret to Zarathustra to the first two lines of Goethe's 'Selige Sehnsucht'. That poem continues 'it is the stuff of life that I want to celebrate (*Das Lebendige will ich preisen*)' — and the next of the three relevant sections of *Thus spake Zarathustra*, namely 'The dancing song', is a rhapsody to 'life': 'I looked recently into your eyes, oh life. And I seemed to be sinking into unfathomable depths'. 'Life', referring to herself as a woman, says she is 'volatile' and 'wild'. Zarathustra is loath to accept this denigrating description, and the reason why he takes a kinder view is expressed by Zarathustra's 'wisdom' — a sort of inner voice, it might seem — when Zarathustra defends 'life' against herself. You are 'full of desire and in love', he is told, 'that is why you praise life'. Zarathustra can but agree, adding a comment that should prompt us to think back to our earlier quotations. When, having conceded his love of 'life', he adds 'and most of all when I hate it', there is the same conjunction of the themes of love and hatred as in the jottings of Nietzsche referred to earlier and in Zarathustra's remarks to the old woman.

We are thus prepared for the enactment of the love–hate relationship between Zarathustra and 'life' which dominates the third of the three sections. This, 'The second dancing song', consists of three numbered parts, of which the first comprises lyrical remarks addressed by Zarathustra to 'life', beginning 'I recently looked into your eyes, oh life', and continuing '... and lust made my heart stand still'. It is an account of a sort of chase, in which Zarathustra and 'life' are seen as lovers, the one making as if to lure the other on, the other withdrawing as if to stimulate desire. Zarathustra can say 'I fear you near me, I fear you at a distance', and yet 'I dance in pursuit of you'. It is a dance 'up hill and down dale' — which is hardly what one would think of as a dance in the proper sense of the term. We might better describe it as a frolic or a gambol. To say that 'she led him a dance', as one could well say of 'life' in respect to Zarathustra, is not to suggest an orderly and rhythmically structured performance, though we shall have to refer to what happens in 'The second dancing song' as a 'dance', if only in inverted commas.

This 'dance' has nothing, for example, to do with those associations of lightness of movement — 'divine ease, agility when most weighed down'[8] — whose ramifications are so important in Nietzsche's philosophy. There is nothing effortless in this 'dance', and we are not surprised to find that both 'life' and Zarathustra are getting tired. Hence Zarathustra's words 'Oh, let me lie down, you wanton creature, and crave mercy! How I would like to go along sweet paths with you ...' Yonder, he says, 'are sheep and sunsets', and how lovely it would be 'to sleep as shepherds pipe'. 'Life' too must be weary, Zarathustra supposes, and he wants to carry her lovingly to her rest — but she is off again. This is more than he can stand. Impatient of being enslaved by her seductiveness, he is now going to make her take orders from him: 'You witch, so far I have sung for you, now *you* shall scream for me!'. His moment of revenge has come, and with it the whip returns to the story. At the moment, that is to say, when he tells 'life' in effect 'thus far and no further', he adds 'and I didn't forget the whip, did I?'.

Obviously then, since this is a reference to the old woman's remark, she and 'life' are one and the same, odd though this personification may seem, bearing in mind the erotic enchantments which characterised the 'dance'. 'Life', so often signifying for Nietzsche the vitalistic ground of existence, hardly lends itself, one might think, to embodiment in the form of one whose time of procreation is over. The personification however is less surprising than might appear if one recalls the equation in *The Birth of Tragedy* of 'life' and 'ancient mother (*Urmutter*)',[9] and the first of the three sections does, after all, juxtapose women old and young. The younger and sexually more attractive creature is the other guise of the old woman in her role as 'life', whom up to that critical point Zarathustra has pursued with such abandon.

It is however not only the reference to the whip that associates 'Of women old and young' and 'The second dancing song'. It is possible to argue that there is a more concealed connection, this being the message that Zarathustra conveys to 'life' in 'The second dancing song', rather as in 'Of women old and young' the old woman imparted one to him. The circumstances are as follows. 'Life', we learn, is jealous of Zarathustra's relationship to 'wisdom' and would dearly like to possess him alone. But she suspects that he is going to prove unfaithful to her. Zarathustra readily admits this, whereupon he whispers something in her ear, just as the old woman had done in his. Her message had been news to him, but, when 'life' hears his, she is merely surprised than somebody other than herself knew about it.

In 'Of women old and young' it is clear, of course, what the secret was, but what Zarathustra confided to 'life' is not revealed. All we have to go on is the fact that immediately afterwards the third and final section of 'The second dancing song' opens with the poem 'Oh man, take heed!', followed by 'The seven seals', with its refrain 'For I love you, oh eternity'. At this point of the book Zarathustra is preoccupied with the idea of eternal recurrence, and we may at least guess that it was this that he mentioned to 'life'. Excited though he might be about it, it was something with which, of course, 'life' was familiar. Moreover, if after disciplining 'life' in the way he did, he still loves her, it is in the knowledge of the pain of parting, and this is caught in the elegiac tone of his words about how he and 'life' looked over 'the green meadow ... and wept together. Then however "life" was dearer to me than all my wisdom'. His message to 'life', we may thus conjecture, included that admixture of joy and suffering which Nietzsche elsewhere sums up in his phrase about joy as 'a sort of pain'. What passed between the two in that confidential moment remains, however, essentially a lover's secret.

A more important question is why Zarathustra is now of a mind to break off his involvement with 'life'. This decision had been reached by the moment when, at the end of the 'dance', he called her — and himself — to order with the whip. A parallel would be with Nietzsche himself in relation to 'décadence', which he had loved with a love comparable to Zarathustra's love of 'life' and which called forth a reaction on his part that enables us to set the one beside the other.

In *The Gay Science* — begun at the end of 1881 and his last work before *Thus spake Zarathustra*, which it pre-dates by only a narrow margin — Nietzsche, talking about the 'magic of life', describes the 'beautiful possibilities' playing around it as 'reluctant', 'bashful', 'seductive', epithets reminiscent of Zarathustra's feelings about 'life' and the way she behaves in 'The second dancing song'. The passage just quoted is entitled 'Vita feminina', and ends with the statement 'yes, life is a woman'.[10] Nietzsche said exactly the same thing about music in *Nietzsche contra Wagner* ('For music ia a woman')[11] — and in *Human, all too Human* he had warned of the need to beware of music, to keep it at a distance. The reason why he compares music to a woman is to be found in those features of it which, he believed, undermine energy and vitality. Thus, for example, in *The Will to Power*, in a discussion of man's will to growth and development towards the state of higher man, he speaks of 'marasmus feminismus'.[12]

With this in mind, it will be useful now to link up our discussion with Nietzsche's criticism of Wagner in *Human, All-too Human*. Modern music, Nietzsche says, thinking of (and quoting) Wagner, aims at 'unending melody'. The effect of this is like when one walks out a little way into the sea, gradually loses one's foothold, 'and surrenders to the water and the waves'.[13] It does not strain the evidence to suggest a parallel with Zarathustra's experience of 'life'. Compare, for example, the notion of sensing the firm ground receding beneath one's feet, with the way, when looking into the eyes of his beloved 'life', he seemed to be sinking 'into the unfathomable'. Zarathustra, of course, is describing a joyous experience; the crisis in his relationship to 'life' is yet to come. But Nietzsche's comments on music date from when his relationship to Wagner had passed breaking-point. Zarathustra is yielding, but Nietzsche has come to the point of resistance. What now appals him is a 'wildness' and 'decay' of rhythm, embodied in a kind of art that 'lacks all proportion'.[14] By contrast with Wagner, Nietzsche argues, hitherto in music 'one had to ... dance'. Typical of music of that kind was the 'keeping of definite and regular grades of tempo and volume', and respect for 'the necessary control', compelling in the soul of the listener a 'constant discretion'.[15] The passage from which these quotations are taken reappears, with slight modifications, in *Nietzsche contra Wagner*, where it comes just before the reference to music as woman. Wagner 'wants a different sort of motion ... swimming, hovering ... but no longer a walk or a dance', and the 'unending melody' aims to break up 'all symmetry and proportion of tempo and volume'.[16] This, as Nietzsche had just said, is more than he can stand, so that at once his foot — which responds to structural order by beating time — 'gets cross' and revolts against Wagner's music, feeling the 'need for rhythm, dance-measure, and the regular beat of the march'.[17]

Now, in the story of the whip, Zarathustra comes to feel much the same need for order — for 'control (*Mass*)' and 'discretion (*Besonnenheit*)' — as Nietzsche now attributes to himself. The comparison seems all the more legitimate, when one remembers the essentially erotic associations in Zarathustra's 'dance' with 'life', and Nietzsche's remark about how he had come to hate the 'nauseating sexuality of Wagner's music'.[18] At the beginning of the 'dance' a rhythmic beat or two from the rattle which 'life' has in her hand starts his feet itching to be on the move, but what follows degenerates, to use Nietzsche's phrase about Wagner, into the 'complete decay of rhythmic feeling', into 'chaos in the place of rhythm'.[19] It was essentially in the name of order and form that Zarathustra rebelled when, unable any longer to tolerate the 'dance' that 'life' had been leading him, he determined to impose order, to prescribe a beat for her to follow, and let her feel the touch of his authority. Decay of rhythm, Nietzsche said, subordinates 'ethos (character, style, or whatever you care to call it)' to mere feeling — and that, he added, is 'décadence'.[20]

With the coming of 'décadence' into the discussion, the implications of the episode of the whip reach their culminating extension. 'To turn my back on Wagner', Nietzsche said, 'was like fate for me', no one 'was perhaps more dangerously tied up with Wagnerianism', 'no one has been more pleased to be rid of it'. Where could one find 'a better initiated leader for the labyrinth of the modern soul, a more eloquent psychologist than Wagner?'. For Nietzsche, Wagner now epitomised 'décadence', and he had discovered that he too was a 'décadent' — with the difference 'that I understood this and resisted it'.[21]

To free himself from Wagner and 'décadence' involved for Nietzsche the discipline of 'self-overcoming', which, together with will to power, is among the central themes of *Thus spake Zarathustra*. The two ideas support each other, as in Nietzsche's remark, applying the will to power to the individual, about the 'power which a genius applies not to his work but to himself ...', and the quotation continues with a reference to the 'taming and purification of his imagination'.[22] This suggests an obvious point of contact with Zarathustra's mood when, combating in himself a self-indulgent weakness of will, he cracks his whip to call 'life', and himself, to order. Weakness of that kind was for Nietzsche incompatible with the obligations of 'self-overcoming' and with achieving the quality of 'higher man'. So, with Zarathustra's flirtation with 'life' in mind, we might think of a note that Nietzsche wrote for the last part of *Thus spake Zarathustra*: 'You want to teach the idea of the Superman — but you have fallen in love with your friends and with yourself, and made life into comfort and refreshment. The islands of happiness make you soft'.[23]

It is moreover very noticeable that, in the episode of the whip, 'life' is devoid of those harsher associations which were to find their most extreme expression, as in *Beyond Good and Evil*, in terms of 'appropriation, wounding, overwhelming of the alien and the weaker, oppression, hardness ... and exploitation'.[24] They were already becoming apparent elsewhere in *Thus spake Zarathustra*, and it is relevant to recall 'The song of the grave', which comes immediately after the middle of the three sections. Its opening motif is 'the graves of my youth', and 'how quickly you died away from me' he says of the 'visions and apparitions of my youth', so that 'today I think of you as my deceased'. How, it is asked, did I bear the destruction of the 'dreams and consolations of my youth', 'how could my soul rise again from these graves?'. Only, Zarathustra says, because of his 'will', in a tribute to which 'The song of the grave' ends: 'Yes, you are still for me the destroyer of all graves: hail to you, my will!'. There remain then only the words 'And where there are graves, there are resurrections' — and, if that does not pick up the theme of 'dying and becoming' in 'Selige Sehnsucht', it is, after what we have said about that poem, a very suggestive coincidence.

The interpretation of the little fable about the old woman and the whip is, as we can now see, a difficult and risky business. It is obviously easier not to ask too many serious questions about it or to push it aside on the excuse that 'that isolated remark' is 'really not so very important', that it is 'perhaps just one of those exaggerated, malicious statements without deeper significance with which Nietzsche likes to spice his discourse'.[25] An alternative way of looking at it, and a much less foolish one, would be to fasten on the section in *Beyond Good and Evil* where, talking about the 'increasing and deadening of most womanly instincts', Nietzsche says that in no previous epoch has woman been treated with such respect by men. Consequently she 'forgets how to fear man', but 'woman who "forgets how to fear" surrenders her most womanly instincts'.[26] That might seem a promising angle on the question of the whip, but in that context it would leave too much unrelated and unexplained to take us very far. There may well be other possible interpretations worth considering, but it would be bold to the point of rashness to expect any of them — including the present one, for that matter — to contain the whole truth and nothing but the truth, the evidence being as elusive as it is.

What is certain is that the mention of the whip has no place in any discussion of Nietzsche's views on the treatment of women as such, and that it cannot be explained in terms of amateur psychology — for example, that 'Nietzsche's attitude to women' and especially 'the fantasies of taking a whip to them' are 'attempts to compensate for his own inadequacy in his personal relations'.[27] Nietzsche's disciples in the feminist movement were thus fully justified in not letting it bother them, even though their reasons were more opportunist than scholarly.

Notes to Appendix

¹ Cf. p. 88.

² According to Hedwig Dohm, the words were not originally Nietzsche's, but 'he quotes them from an old Florentine story the saying: "Buona femina e mala feminina vuol bastone'. (The good and the evil woman deserve the stick)'. Cf. *Die Antifeministen* (Berlin, 1916, Paperback reprint, Frankfurt am Main, 1976), p. 30.

³ *Kritische Ausgabe*, VII/1, pp. 97–8.

⁴ C. A. Bernoulli, *Franz Overbeck und Friedrich Nietzsche* I (Jena, 1908), p. 338.

⁵ Cf. Ernst Pfeiffer (ed.), *Friedrich Nietzsche, Paul Rée, Lou von Salomé: die Dokumente ihrer Begegnung* (Frankfurt am Main, 1970), pp. 190 ff.

⁶ *Kritische Ausgabe*, VII/1, p. 36.

⁷ Max Nettlau, *Die historische Entwicklung des Anarchismus 1895–1914*, Part I, p. 156. Unpublished, in the Max Nettlau Archiv at the Institute of Social History, Amsterdam.

⁸ *Werke*, III, p. 441.

⁹ *Ibid.*, I, p. 93.

¹⁰ *Ibid.*, II, p. 201.

¹¹ *Ibid.*, II, p. 1045.

¹² *Ibid.*, III, p. 471.

¹³ *Ibid.*, I, p. 788.

¹⁴ *Ibid.*, I, p. 789.

¹⁵ *Ibid.*, I, p. 788.

¹⁶ *Ibid.*, II, p. 1043.

¹⁷ *Ibid.*, II, p. 1041.

¹⁸ Letter to Malwida von Meysenbug, 1888. Cf. Janz, *op. cit.*, I, p. 505.

¹⁹ *Werke*, II, p. 1043.

²⁰ *Ibid.*, III, p. 1226.

²¹ *Ibid.*, II, pp. 903–4.

²² *Ibid.*, I, p. 1269.

²³ *Kritische Ausgabe*, VII/1, p. 558.

²⁴ *Werke*, II, p. 729.

²⁵ H. Meyer-Benfey, 'Nietzsche und die Liebe', in *Welt und Dichtung* (Hamburg-Wandsbek, n. d.).

²⁶ *Werke*, II, p. 701.

²⁷ *The Oxford Companion to German Literature* (Oxford, 1976), p. 505.

Select Bibliography

Brinton, Crane, *Nietzsche*, Cambridge, Mass., 1941.

Coplestone, F., *Friedrich Nietzsche: Philosopher of Culture*, London and New York, 1975.

Diesz, Gisela, *Die Entwicklung des Nietzsche-Bildes in Deutschland*, Würzburg, 1933.

Hayman, Ronald, *Nietzsche: a Critical Life*, London, 1980.

Heller, Peter, *Dialectics and Nihilism*, University of Massachusetts Press, 1966.

Hillebrand, Bruno (ed.), *Nietzsche und die deutsche Literatur*, 2 vols. (I) *Texte zur Nietzsche-Rezeption* II *Forschungsergebnisse*, Munich, 1978 and Tübingen, 1978.

Hollingdale, R. J., *Nietzsche: The Man and his Philosophy*, Baton Rouge and London, 1965.

Hollingdale, R. J., *Nietzsche*, London, 1973.

Hollingdale, R. J., *A Nietzsche Reader* London, 1977.

Janz, C. P., *Friedrich Nietzsche: Biographie*, 3 vols., Munich, 1978, 1979.

Jaspers, K., *Nietzsche: an Introduction to the Understanding of his Philosophical Activity*, Chicago, 1965.

Kaufmann, Walter, *Nietzsche*, Princeton, 1950.

Lea, F. A., *The Tragic Philosopher: a Study of Friedrich Nietzsche*, New York, 1957.

Mann, Thomas, *Nietzsches Philosophie im Lichte unserer Erfahrung*, Berlin, 1948.

Pasley, Malcolm (ed.), *Nietzsche: Imagery and Thought*, London, 1978.

Prinzhorn, Hans, *Nietzsche und das XX. Jahrhundert*, Heidelberg, 1928.

Ross, Werner, *Der ängstliche Adler: Friedrich Nietzsches Leben* Stuttgart, 1980.

Steffen, Hans (ed.), *Nietzsche: Werk und Wirkungen*, Göttingen, 1974.

Stern, J. P., *Nietzsche*, London, 1978.

Stern, J. P., *A Study of Nietzsche*, Cambridge, 1979.

For historical reference

Craig, Gordon A., *Germany 1966–1945*, Oxford, 1978.

Flenley, Ralph, *Modern German History*, London, 1953.

Holborn, Hajo, *A History of Modern Germany 1840–1945*, London, 1969.

Mann, G. I., *The History of Germany since 1789*, (London, 1968).

Index